The Island's True Child

∿

The
Island's
True Child

A Memoir of Growing Up on Criehaven

~

Dorothy Simpson

With additional text by her niece
Dorothy Elisabeth Simpson

Afterword by Elisabeth Ogilvie

2   4   5   3   1

DOWN EAST BOOKS
A Division of Down East Enterprise, Inc.,
publisher of Down East magazine

Orders: 1-800-766-1670

www.downeastbooks.com

To my best friend and kindred spirit, Lil,
who has always been there for me.
Without her support, this book
would not have come to be.

༄

This work is also dedicated to the memory
of Aleda Dorothy Knowlton Simpson,
my Aunt Dot, whose stories of her youth
always kept me wanting to hear more.
What a gift she gave our family
by putting her words to paper.

D.E.S.

Contents ∿

Acknowledgments ~

I would like to thank the people who helped me to complete this project. My editor, Karin Womer, read over the manuscript and immediately appreciated it as much as I did; without her guidance and suggestions I would have been lost. Melissa Hayes retyped Aunt Dot's original manuscript into digital files, deciphering the typos and helping to smooth the wording as needed. Her input has been very important in making this book a successful family heirloom.

Particular thanks go to my best friend, Lil (Callahan) Oldham, who persuaded me to follow my heart, and to my Mom, Winnifred Simpson, who has been a constant support and story collaborator.

I also want to thank my children and their families for being so patient with me while I spent so much time working on this book. I labored over this project so they would have this gift of family history.

Many family members and friends contributed photos or supportive information: Barbara Ogilvie Mosher helped me obtain Aunt Dot's writings and photos; my cousins Esther Ann (Simpson) Darres, Ruth Elmina (Simpson) Schroeder, Donald Simpson, Dennis Young, Rosemary (Young) Elliot, Shirley (Simpson) Ruminski, Mary Ellen (Brown) Britts, and Jean Crie Hodgkins all took the time to talk with me about Aunt Dot's family and also shared family photos.

Special thanks also go to Elisabeth Ogilvie, Aunt Liz, for sharing her and Aunt Dot's photo collection—often helping me figure out who was who in the pictures—and for writing the Afterword to this book. She has always shared my love for "the island" and my family. She has been my connection to Aunt Dot and to Criehaven since Aunt Dot passed away. Without her, I would be lonely. —*D.E.S.*

Aunt Dot as I Knew Her ~

Dorothy Elisabeth Simpson

I was the middle child of five, and the third of four daughters, in a Criehaven lobsterman's family. I often wondered why I was the one given the honor of being named after two great women, and I always felt a connection to both of my namesakes. Like them, I have always loved the island, the ocean, the outdoors, and the sense of freedom that comes from dwelling in a place that makes you feel complete.

I was named after my Aunt Dorothy Simpson and Elisabeth Ogilvie, both accomplished writers. Elisabeth is the well-known author of more than fifty novels, most of them set in Maine or the Scottish Highlands. For my sisters and me, Elisabeth has always been "Aunt Liz," though there is no blood relationship. Many of her best-loved novels are based on the families of Criehaven (Ragged Island*), where Aunt Dot grew up and Elisabeth's family spent summers. Dot and Elisabeth became fast friends despite a twelve-year difference in age, and their shared love for Criehaven and the written word kept them close until Dot's death in 1998. For years after they left Criehaven, in 1944, they both wrote movingly of that remote island and its vanishing way of life.

I spent a great deal of time with Aunt Dot and Aunt Liz over the

---

*According to the mapmakers, Criehaven is the settlement on Ragged Island, but most people simply call the island Criehaven.

years, but 1972, the year I graduated from high school, particularly stands out in my memory because I stayed at their house on Gay's Island for the summer. That was first time I spent weeks away from my family. There I got to do things that I'd never been allowed to do when I was at home on Criehaven with my parents. Dot and Liz let me have my own lobster traps. I could go out in a boat whenever I wanted. I could fish, dig for clams, and explore the islands and just be a free spirit. Aunt Dot taught me how to knit trap heads and to make her favorite fudge, and she encouraged me to browse through the many books she and Aunt Liz owned.

Other wonderful memories are from 1961, when Aunt Dot and Aunt Liz took care of me and my two older sisters, Joyce and Paula. We were all of school age, and because there was no longer a school on the island, we lived with Liz and Dot in their winter house on the mainland while our parents remained on Criehaven. During our stay in Cushing, my sisters and I were introduced to many new experiences, from listening to Scottish music, to painting by numbers, to learning to play the ukulele. A creative person herself, Aunt Dot wanted us to explore all aspects of life. She'd taught herself to play the fiddle, organ, tenor guitar, baritone ukulele, and banjo. My father also played the guitar, so Dot was very excited to have the opportunity to teach his daughters to play ukulele. We loved it, and my father was very touched when we surprised him with a concert.

It was some time later that Aunt Liz added our characters to one of her many novels. She'd so enjoyed our antics and adventures that she wanted to share them with her readers. The book was *Waters on a Starry Night* (published 1968), and my character's name is Chris.

Ever since that visit, I was drawn to Aunt Dot. I didn't know why then, but discovered as a teen that it was because we were kindred spirits. I was also quite the tomboy and wanted to do all the fun things the boys did: haul lobster traps, fill bait bags, go rowing, build traps, etc. We both grew up in a family of lobstermen. We both loved the ocean and boats. Aunt Dot never let the fact that she was a woman in a man's world stop her from educating herself in writing, music, and painting. When she was growing up, it was not common for girls to help with knitting trap heads, filling bait-bags, or painting buoys, but Aunt Dot wanted to do *all* that her Papa and brothers were able to do. After moving to Cushing, she kept her own boat and lobster traps and owned several parcels of land on the mainland and on Gay's Island.

She always amazed me with her strength of character and her passion to work hard for what she wanted. Aunt Dot was tough when need be, yet generous beyond reason to family and friends; many a time her heart was broken by the acts of ungrateful family members. It wasn't until after her death, when I read her unpublished writings, that I realized her unspoken devotion for her family, friends, island life, animals, nature, music, art, and poetry.

Over the years, I'd often listened to Aunt Dot talk about my grand-father and grandmother and other family members I'd never had the chance to meet. I later rediscovered those tales in written form when I acquired her papers: journals, pages of poetry, stories of her life after her father died, fiction about World War II, and romances apparently written with the day's popular magazines in mind.

As wonderful as my own childhood on Criehaven was, I do be-lieve that Aunt Dot's was far more incredible. *The Island's True Child* will give you an idea of the adventures, the simple happiness, and the sorrows that my aunt experienced as a girl and young woman living in a remote, traditional fishing community. She wrote it as a tribute to the person she most admired—her Papa, an honest, fair, patient, and lov-ing man, who was rich in humanity if not in worldly possessions. Even though she thought she was mostly writing about her father, it really is a narrative about young Dot herself.

As you read, you will be caught up in Aunt Dot's spirit, her pas-sion for the sea, and her sense of adventure. She had a thirst for knowl-edge, and became an avid reader as soon as she could start sounding out the words on the page. With the support of her father, she was allowed to read as often as she could find the free time. While still a teenager—again with her father's encouragement—she began to write stories and dream of being a professional writer.

Aunt Dot did publish several books and articles in time, and thank goodness she kept all or most of her unpublished writings as well. When she died, she left her papers to Aunt Elisabeth, who generously agreed to turn them over to me to keep them in the family. I took home a large box of letters, old manuscripts, journals dating back to the 1930s, and wonderful tales about growing up on Criehaven, including this memoir. I was so moved by this story of my grandfather and his family that I had to share it with others.

Because Aunt Dot was such a skilled writer, we had to do very little to get her manuscript into publishable shape. We changed a word or moved a comma here and there and did our best to decipher the lines of typed-over text. We've also added a few explanatory notes and made dates more specific where possible. I wish Aunt Dot were still here so I could ask her about certain people and events that are, curiously, not mentioned in these pages. Dot brought back to life a world so intriguing that we just naturally wish we could see more of it.

In the preceding pages I've touched on just a few of my thoughts about my Aunt Dot and what a mentor she was to me. Similarly, the memoir you are about to read only touches on some of Dot's many experiences as an island child, and it ends when she is barely thirty. I write briefly about her later life in a concluding chapter, but first, here is Aleda Dorothy Knowlton Simpson's own story, told in her own way. I know you will enjoy it.

"For me, Criehaven is an island not so much in
a geographical sense but in a spiritual sense,
for I can carry it with me wherever I go....
I have not deserted Criehaven. Neither has Dot,
who in blood and bone is the island's true
child. Each of us has taken it with her, and it
will be with us for the rest of our lives."

—Elisabeth Ogilvie, *My World Is an Island,* 1950

Village of Criehaven

Places where Dot's family lived

1 Herman roomed on second floor of beach workshop

2 Camp Herman shared with two other bachelor fishermen

3 Small house Herman owned at the time he married

4 Grandparents' house, where family lived briefly after returning from Vinalhaven in 1912

5 Simpsons rented two-room apartment from 1913 to 1918

6 Small house near the ocean, rented from 1918 to 1922

7 Moved to large apartment in "The Beehive" in 1922.

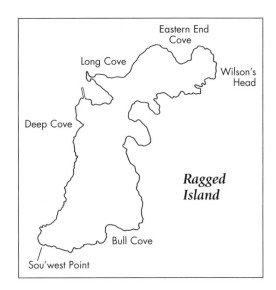

Ragged Island

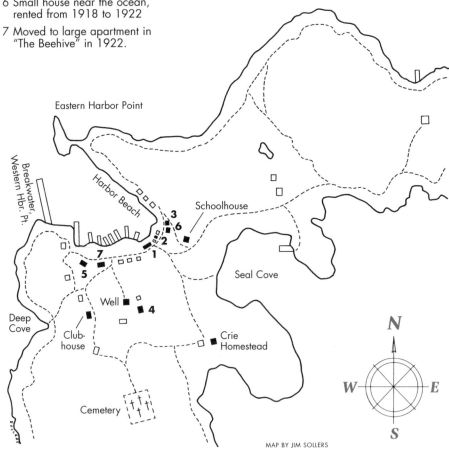

MAP BY JIM SOLLERS

The Island's True Child

On the breast of the Atlantic
In the mouth of the Penobscot,
Lies a tiny little island;
Just a bit of field and forest,
Just a bit of sand and ledges—
Ledges where the crying sea gulls
Nest and nurture their wild fledglings.

Underneath the summer sunshine,
On this atom of God's pleasure,
Live and love some forty people.
People who are not unusual;
Fishermen and wives and children—
Children that will grow to manhood
Filled with love for this small island.

They all have their faults and errors,
Imperfections, flaws, and failings,
But they're God's own, "in his image,"
And as such they know His blessings—
Blessings that are placed upon them
As they live and know each other
On this tiny wave-washed islet.

༄

From "Criehaven," by Dorothy Simpson,
written sometime in the 1930s.

The Gentle Eagle ~

In the late 1800s, Fred, Alfred, and Herman Simpson set sail from the town of Bucksport, Maine, in a fishing dory. The dory was equipped with a tiny sail, two pairs of oars, some food and water, and some extra clothing. They were going down the Penobscot River, taking advantage of the current, using the sail when there was breeze enough, and fastening on the oars when they were becalmed. They were going out into the bay, beyond Owls Head, beyond the reach of the Mussel Ridge chain of islands, until they came to the little group of islands twenty-five miles south of Rockland, of which Matinicus is the largest. But they were not stopping at Matinicus; they were going on to the next largest island. South Matinicus it was called then. Criehaven it is called today. On the nautical charts it is Ragged Island. And I have been told that the Indians called it Racketash.

Fred and Alfred were the older brothers, and they had seen Ragged Island many times when they were on board the fishing schooners that were bound for the Grand Banks. They had looked at Ragged Island lying in the distance, capped with blue-green spruce above rocky shores that gleamed for miles in sunlight, and had learned, somehow, that a man could go handlining in a dory from there, and sell his catch at the Crie wharf, and rent a camp where he could eat and sleep, and feel the good solid earth under him when he was through with his work.

It had sounded good to Fred and Alfred, so they had decided to make a try at it. They were tall, big, rawboned men with deep-set eyes and strong jaws. They had spent winters in the lumber camps of northern Maine and summers on the fishing schooners. It seemed to them that they were well equipped for living on Ragged Island and going handlining in the dory that was bringing them down from Bucksport on this beautiful day.

Herman was the youngest brother. He had been in the lumber camps too, but not on the Grand Banks. He was going to Ragged Island not to handline but to be the cook and housekeeper for his older brothers. He was nineteen, tall and rangy like the others, with the same deep-set eyes, but his jaw was not so thick and square. His face was more narrow, but that didn't soften the effect of the thin, strong, aquiline nose or take away the bleak, icy look that could sometimes come into the blue eyes.

They arrived at Ragged Island without mishap, and were shown to a place where they could live and keep their gear. The shore of the little harbor was high on one side, walled with the tawny red rock that could shine so brightly in a certain light. The other side was low and flat, with a wide, gleaming, rocky beach that sloped up gently from the water to meet the marsh. On the flat side were the camps and fish houses and the big wharf where the Crie family carried on the business of handling salt fish, curing it and storing it until schooners came from Boston to take it off their hands at a fine profit.

Herman did more than cook and sweep and wash; when Fred and Alfred came in with a doryload of fish, he climbed into his oil-pants and helped to cut off fish heads, take out the insides, and then carry the split fish to the weighing scales.

The three brothers must have done exceedingly well, for in due time Fred and Alfred were able to buy a number of acres of land at the most eastern point of the island, where they could have gardens, a cow, pigs, chickens, and all the things they wanted to make a real home. Moreover, the Eastern End was remote and wildly beautiful. Cut off from the rest of the island by a thick belt of woods, and with water on three sides and a towering stand of spruce on the fourth side, they could maintain a certain aloofness and solitude. By this time they must have been tired of living in the huddle of camps on the beach at the harbor.

When Fred and Alfred went back upriver for their wives, Herman didn't leave Ragged Island. He stayed and went on fishing for the Cries. This must have been a lucrative business during these years, because in time Herman bought himself a small house near the edge of the harbor shore, away from the camps but so close to the water that the sound of it was always in the house, even the softest whisper it makes on a still summer evening.

Herman didn't get married until he was in his mid-thirties. He owned property, he was industrious, he was tall and lean and straight as an Indian; he had fine, penetrating blue eyes and a fair mustache, which he always kept sprucely groomed. He must have been a good prospect, but for some reason he remained single until he met Agnes Anderson Knowlton, a young girl who had already married and had a child, but her husband had gone away before the child was born. When her daughter was two and a half, the twenty-year-old Scandinavian girl with the thick brown hair and round hazel eyes married Herman Simpson.

Thus he became my stepfather. And when I was old enough to listen to the tales he liked to tell, he would talk to me about the time the brothers set out from Bucksport for Ragged Island, and how they had never gone away from the island since.

My first memories of Papa were tied up with the little white house he owned, the sound of the surf on the pebbled beach below; the smell of his clay pipe; the drooping yellow mustache that hid his upper lip; the bright, dancing light of the harbor waters when the sun was in the west, filling the front room with ruddy-gold radiance; and the teddy bear without which I could never go to bed.

I have been told many things about that time, but I do not remember them, except that with the telling they seem very familiar. I was a little, stubby child, fat and round-faced, with a firm mouth and an unquenchably stubborn disposition. I marvel now at Papa's patience. I have been told how I painted the sitting room stove with his yellow buoy paint, which he stored in the woodshed during the summer months, and how I drank kerosene from a can standing on the shed floor. I was adept at eating the burned ends of matches and the soft, crumbly pieces of coal ashes, and eggshells, and plaster from the walls if I could work some loose. Nowadays they say it's a dietary deficiency that causes such goings-on, but in those days it was just another sign of my unpredictable nature. I was always falling down and bumping my head on the big, flat rocks that made up our back yard. I can't remember any of these things, but it seems I spent more time rolling and howling than I did walking.

But I do remember how I loved to play with an old broken-bladed jackknife that was once Papa's, and a clean white clay pipe with its stem broken so short he could not use it. And I remember how his mother, a tall, rawboned, fierce-eyed woman with tight lips, found me playing with these treasures once when she was visiting us and took them away from me, throwing them overboard with the reprimand that little girls didn't play with things like that. I got even with her, for in later years I learned how to use Papa's good knife and could whittle out boats to sail in saltwater puddles, sharpen pencils to beautiful points, and make whistles from the alder bushes. I never aspired to smoke his pipe, though. I guess I knew it would make me sick. I did roll up dried birch leaves into pretty good cigars, and when I got into the house I had to try to explain away the smell that clung to me; Papa was always afraid I had been building a fire in the woods.

What I have learned of the life of the fisherman on the Maine coast began with his teachings. He was never too tired to explain things to me, or too annoyed when I didn't learn quickly.

He was not a coward or a bully, and he was always trying to impress upon me his principles of tolerance and fair play. He hated liars and cheats, but his dislike was evident only in the way he avoided them. Any hint of stealing would make him most severe. If any of us children brought home anything that we had found "just lying around," we would have to march it back and put it where we found it. The only things we could bring home were the things we found washed ashore by the tide. That was one of the joys of beachcombing—we didn't have to take anything back again and put it where we found it.

When I look back and compare him with his brothers, and remember the rocklike strength of his mother's face, and then think of the years that I wandered around in Papa's wake, watching him, listening to his yarns and his philosophy, I wonder what made the difference in him. The other brothers had the same long faces with the deep-set eyes—eyes that could pierce you like knives—and the grim mouths above the strong chins. Like him, they had big fists and long, strong arms, and long legs that could step nimbly into a dory. Fred had a strong, deep voice that could roar with a threat one moment and then go off into the sweet tones of an Irish ballad the next. Alfred's voice was not as deep as Fred's, and I never heard him sing, but his voice was not one you would trifle with, no matter if it was softer than Fred's. Papa's voice was softer still, and when he sang it was not loud, but it was a right voice for lulling a child as he held it on his knee or moved the cradle with his toe.

Other men of the island were strong too, but there were only a couple more that were as big. The others were shorter men—some broad and stubby, others slight and trim. But the three Simpson brothers were of a breed apart, it seemed to me. That they had come from up the Penobscot River added to that apartness. And the way they could talk about the big forests of Maine, the logging crews, the drives downriver in the spring—it all gave them an atmosphere that none of the other men had.

My maternal grandfather came from Norway. He had run away at the age of eleven to sail the seven seas and eventually ended up on Ragged Island with his family of five children. I had an uncle who had been born in Copenhagen and had received his education on a school ship. He had sailed on the White Star Line for years and was now on Ragged Island as a fisherman and boatbuilder. The Crie family were Scottish and could trace their ancestry back to the time when the first Crie came to this country. He had been a shoemaker in Scotland and had been pressed into service, then deserted from the British army when they landed at Castine. There were other men with romantic backgrounds too, but somehow the three who came from upriver, who had been a part of the big forests, and who carried their fair heads so arrogantly, their mustaches with such an air, and their shoulders so squarely, topped all the rest.

In my childish imagination I saw them as eagles who had come down from the wilderness to settle on the rocky shores of Ragged Island, to turn their cold, bright eyes on whatever moved or stood, and by the strength of their minds and bodies hold what was theirs against all the storms that broke in fury over the island.

And because Papa had a different look around his jaw and chin, and a softer sound to his voice, and a way of forgiveness that the others didn't have, I came to see him a little differently. He was an eagle too—he had the look of one—but he was a gentle eagle.

Papa's Light ~

In 1911 Papa moved us—my mother, my younger brother Donald and sister Ruth, and me—from Ragged Island to Vinalhaven, an island about fifteen miles to the northeast. It was so much larger than Ragged Island or Matinicus that it didn't seem like an island at all, but like mainland. There were sidewalks on the main street, and some people were beginning to think of having automobiles. My first ride in a car was with our newly acquainted family doctor. A young man, he was tall and thin and dark, and to me he was as romantic as his red roadster. I would have thought him the most wonderful man in the world, next to Papa, if it hadn't been for the new baby that eventually arrived to complicate my existence. I thought it was entirely unnecessary of the doctor to bring it to us when we had enough babies in the family already.

It was on Vinalhaven that I first attended school and discovered the rapture of printed words, clean, new paper, and freshly sharpened pencils.

Papa intended to go lobstering as he had done at Ragged Island, but instead he went fishing for halibut in a tubby little schooner called the *Paul Jones.* Instead of being at home with us every night, he was away for two weeks at a time. But it meant earning money for us, so we got along the best we could while he was gone.

He rented a house that was close to the shore of a creek that wound in from the sea. When the tide was high, it touched the grassy sloping banks, and when it was low, the creek was a lovely stretch of clam flats where the gulls and crows strolled and argued noisily over a morsel of food.

We children were never allowed near the shore, and so of course the grassy banks and the mudflats were the most fascinating places imaginable. When the creek brimmed over with high tide, it fascinated us in a different way. We had the sea in our blood, and we were drawn irrevocably to the water. Day after day we ran off to the creek, and got either wet or muddy—according to the tide—and were severely punished. At the time the punishments seemed unjust, but now when I look back I can see why we needed them. With Papa away so much, and Mama not feeling so good with a baby coming—which, of course, I didn't know about—she had to be stern with us. Certainly she didn't want Papa coming home from fishing to learn that one of us had been drowned.

At that time the shore along the creek was not thickly settled, and our few neighbors had no children. I saw no one my age except when I went to school, but I was too shy to make friends. My brother Donald, being close to me in age, was all right to play with, but little Ruth was just learning to walk, so she was not much fun. She was a nuisance: someone I had to watch, and someone who needed plenty of watching. She had an unfailing instinct for Getting Into Things.

The four of us managed fairly well with Papa gone so many days at a time, but it was always a happy event when he returned to us. His presence seemed to light the house as if he brought a strange kind of lamp with him, and there was laughter and much talking because he'd have to tell Mama about the fishing trip. If it had been a good one he was very gay. He would fool with us—trot us on his knee, tickle our necks, and ask silly riddles—and he would hug Mama hard and make her squirm to get away from him.

We'd have to tell him how we'd behaved: if we'd been good, how good? And if bad, how bad? If we'd been very bad, he would frown and look very angry. His heavy eyebrows would come down over his blue eyes, his long mustache would seem to bristle fiercely, and his thin aquiline nose and long bony face would make me think of an eagle's, and I would be afraid. But only for a moment, for then he would speak, and his voice was not like the sharpness of his face or the glitter of his eyes. It was a soft voice that tried to sound severe but instead sounded kind. Then his big hands would reach out and draw us to him, and my brother and I would be deeply ashamed of having been so bad. We would promise, desperately contrite, to do better next time.

As soon as the promise was made, his eyebrows would go back into place, his eyes would soften and his mustache unbristle, and he'd reach into his pocket and give us a penny and tell us to run along to the store for a piece of candy. The store was a long way off for my short, plump legs and Donald's much shorter ones, and it was up a hill, but he'd tell us not to hurry. He'd look at Mama with a twinkle, and when Donald and I left the house he'd tell us not to get taken by the Indians. We'd know he was joking; no Indians lived anywhere around.

The long walk to the store did not seem too long, even when I had to hold Donald's hand and toil up the hill, for we knew there'd be candy at the end of it.

The harbor where Papa had to go to board the *Paul Jones* was farther down the same road, and after he'd been gone the usual length of time, my brother and I would take turns watching for him to come down the dusty track. We could see him when he was still a long way off, and Mama might let us go to meet him, unless it was storming. On those days, we'd stand by the window and watch him coming, his long legs growing longer and his head growing higher as he neared the house. He always walked like a soldier marching, and I used to wonder if he heard drums and fifes and saw flags flying in his mind as he measured the road home.

One sunny day when a strong wind made the gulls rise high against the sky and circle round and round as if they were hung on invisible strings, my brother and I stood watching for Papa while Mama was busy in the kitchen making something good for supper. Baby Ruth was asleep in her daytime bed—a couch in the sitting room with a chair backed against it so she couldn't roll out—and everything was quiet except for Mama moving around in the kitchen.

I was watching the road intently, so I failed to notice that Donald's attention had wandered and that he was examining something in the corner behind me. It was an object we had been cautioned over and over not to touch, and I stood in great terror of it, because I fully believed it could set the house on fire.

It was actually a fire extinguisher, but the word *extinguisher* sounded very violent to me. No one had ever bothered to explain what it really meant. The thing always stood upright in its corner, with its small hose hanging at its side, and I had never known any yearning to touch it, even lightly. But Donald was curious and never satisfied with things as they were, so while I watched the road and Mama's eyes were on her cooking, Donald knocked over the fire extinguisher. I heard the noise, and when I turned to look I was horror-stricken at the sight of the liquid coming from the nozzle of the hose and running out on the floor. I went into a panic.

"The house is on fire!" I shrieked.

Mama came running, and the baby awoke with a howl. I looked out the window and saw a tall, familiar figure coming down the road. It was Papa! But he should hurry! He should be running, or the house would be too far gone in flames before he could save us! I was in a frenzy of excitement.

Without a glance toward Mama to see what she might be doing to save the day, I dashed out of the house and down the road as fast as my fat legs would take me. But as fast as they went, I wanted to go faster; the devil of fear was driving me on. My breath burned in my throat and chest, and my legs ached so I could hardly move them, but I managed to keep going and to keep crying out, "Hurry, Papa! The house is on fire!"

When he realized I was not rushing and crying out from joy, he ran to meet me, and as soon as he touched me I collapsed in the road. He picked me up in his arms and kept running on toward the house. I was too overcome with fear and exhaustion to care what happened next, but he seemed to fly along as if his feet wore wings instead of rubber boots. Then we were at the door and Mama was saying matter-of-factly, "There's nothing the trouble. Donald upset the extinguisher, and she thought it had set the house on fire."

Papa set me down, and I looked around unbelievingly. In my imagination I had heard flames crackling behind me as I'd bolted from the house. In my mad race down the road I hadn't dared to turn my head to see how much progress the fire had made, and now I felt rather dazed, as if awakening from a bad dream. The fire extinguisher stood in its usual fashion in the corner; there was no liquid on the floor. Donald stood grinning at me, his chubby face and blue eyes under the yellow bangs all aglow with the excitement he had caused. And there was no fire at all. Nothing was changed.

I looked at Papa, and he was smiling at me, and suddenly I began to cry and shake all over. I reached for him, sobbing, "Rock me, Papa. Rock me!" That was the one balm I knew for all my childhood sufferings. And without stopping to take off his jacket and hat, he took me on his lap and rocked me till the tears had dried and the shivering stopped. Then he explained how the extinguisher really worked, and why we children should never touch it. If we tipped it over some time when Mama was not around to know we had done it, and all the fluid was lost, and then later the house *really* caught fire, the extinguisher would be no good. Mama would not be able to put the fire out at all. While he talked his hand patted my shoulder, and his voice was very gentle and his eyes were very soft.

When I was entirely quieted, he set me down and took off his hat and jacket. I saw him look at Donald. His eyebrows came down fiercely, and his mustache bristled up to meet them, and his nose and chin grew very sharp.

"I hate to do this, son," he said. He reached for my little brother and laid him across his knees to spank him with his big brown hand. "But you've got to learn to leave things like that alone." He spanked hard, and Donald cried hard, and then Papa stood him on his feet and said, "Think you can remember now?"

Through his tears and sobbing Donald mumbled, "Yes."

Papa looked at us three, Donald, Mama, and then me, and said in the voice that was always easy no matter how savage his face looked, "Well, I guess we can have supper now, can't we?"

While Mama set Donald and me up to the table, he went in and took up our baby sister and brought her out to sit on his knee through the meal. While we ate there was much talking and laughing, and over us all was that light that Papa carried with him wherever he went, and his face was like an eagle's still, but it didn't make us afraid—its expression was too happy and content.

The Turnip Tops ~

When I was seven, we moved from Vinalhaven back to the smaller island whence we had made our first migration. The new baby had arrived [on September 12], a boy, and Papa was tired of fishing for halibut. So the tubby schooner that had carried the halibut he'd caught now carried all our belongings back to Criehaven. It was in the fall, and we had no place to go except into my mother's father's house, a house that was very small, and into which we fitted too snugly. But as that was all the roof we could get under, we were glad to be there, even if it meant living with my grandfather, who was a very short-tempered man and given to sarcastic observations without much notice beforehand.

I can't recall just where all our belongings were stored, but probably in Grandpa's woodshed, which was quite a large building—more of a workshop, storehouse, and milk-room combined. My grandfather was Swedish-Norwegian, meaning that he was born in Norway, but spoke Swedish and talked about Sweden more than he did about Norway. He had run away from home at a very early age and had been around the world on square-riggers before he had reached his teens, and he used all the tricks he'd learned from the bucko mates of those days to keep his little home and family in order.

He had little use for the way Papa had sold his house and moved to Vinalhaven, and less use for the way he had come back, with a new mouth to feed and no roof to cover us. He was not enthusiastic over the fact that he'd had to offer us his home. He was not at all backward in letting Papa know how he felt about things, at every opportunity.

Anyway, we filled the little house almost to bursting, and there wasn't much in the way of privacy, so that when Oram, the baby, cried at night, everybody in the house knew of it.

Maybe boy babies are louder than girl babies because they are developing lung power that they must use later in giving orders and laughing loud when they feel good. Certainly, when he woke up in the night with a pain in his stomach, this new little brother of mine could yell strong enough almost to lift the shingles off the roof above us. And for some reason Oram could not be quieted, so Papa would have to get up and walk the floor with him, and pat his back, and go downstairs and heat water, and give him paregoric to quiet him.

In the meantime everyone else would be awakened and twisting their heads on their pillows, trying to get away from the baby's crying. Somehow nothing else can work its way into your ears like the sound of a baby crying at night—the kind of crying that goes on and on and on, with a monotony of tone that makes you want to sit up and scream too. So by the time Papa would get back to bed with the baby quiet in his arms, nobody else felt like settling down. Little pale streaks of daylight would be edging the drawn curtains when everybody else at last relaxed enough to sleep again, but that was the hour when Grandpa always arose to do the chores that stood in his way before he could eat his breakfast and go haul his lobster traps.

Grandpa had a little farm to help make his lobstery pay. Actually, he had a *tiny* farm. About two acres of land looking pleasantly across the harbor toward Matinicus and walled by the woods behind were given up to fields for his hay, his garden, his barnyard, his cherry orchard, and his house and its yards. In his barn he kept a cow, a calf, a pig, chickens, a collie dog, and a cat. Sometimes he had ducks and a goose or two on hand for Thanksgiving and Christmas. What Grandpa earned from his lobster pots, therefore, could be put away for other things beside food.

His little farm kept him far busier than if he had been just a plain lobster fisherman, and when he was kept awake half the night by a baby howling out of sheer perversity—that was the way Grandpa regarded it—he was in no mood for trifling, and nobody dared speak to him except with the deepest respect.

Papa's disposition was being tried severely too, and at the same time he was decidedly worried by the fact that this baby boy of his had not cried on Vinalhaven the way he was crying on Criehaven. Papa thought of everything a man could think of that might make a baby cry the way Oram was doing. He asked Mama if she had given him anything during the day that might have upset him. Mama bridled at that; she wasn't in the habit of giving children things to upset them. She gave them milk. The others had had her own milk, but the new baby had cow's milk, and that was certainly a good food for a child. No one could dispute that.

Papa didn't offer to dispute it. He thought deeply about it, though, and then he began to talk about it, and finally he asked Grandpa what he fed his cow. He asked politely enough, but there was something about the inquiry—Papa's dignity, perhaps—that Grandpa took as an insult. What did Herman intimate by such a question? He drew himself up to the fullest of his short, spare height, his thick, dark beard jutting forward, and looked up at my father, who was looking down at him with his eyebrows very thick over his eyes. Grandpa had a way of sniffing that could sound almost as sarcastic as anything he might say, and now he sniffed eloquently, rocked forward on his toes, and stuck his thumbs under his suspenders, waiting for Papa to explain what he meant by such a question.

Very patiently and quietly, Papa said that perhaps it was something the cow had eaten that was causing Oram to cry nights. To be frank, Papa said, he thought the baby had colic, and colic was gas, and gas was very painful, and fairly tied the baby up in knots. It was a full and complete explanation that Papa gave, and to me, listening with great admiration, it sounded very sensible and very finely put, but to Grandpa it was an insult to both the cow and himself.

It meant he had to watch everything he gave his cow if he wanted to be sure of a good night's sleep. And Grandpa was not in the habit of catering to *anyone's* appetites and foibles, much less a baby's. So he drew himself up even taller, and pulled his suspender straps way out, teetered on his toes, and stuck his chin—and beard—up toward Papa. He said very loudly that he had nothing to do with the baby's crying. His cow had nothing to do with it. In fact, it was entirely the baby's fault that he cried, and while he thought of it, he wanted to add that he was sick of being kept awake all night.

Papa agreed with him on that point. He said that everybody was sick of being kept awake, and nobody was feeling any worse than the baby was. Papa said it was a terrible thing for a baby to suffer so, and he was going to get to the reason for it. And with that remark, he turned on his heel and walked away from Grandpa, who looked after him with something very like a sneer.

For a long time, it seemed, Papa could not discover the reason for Oram's spells of colic, but then one day he happened to walk into the barn just as Grandpa was tossing turnip tops into the cow's crib. He stood and watched her munching the hardy green leaves with all the gusto a cow can manage, and then he looked at Grandpa, who was cleaning out the back of her stall. I waited, hopefully.

"Andrew,"* said Papa quietly, "how long you been feeding that cow turnip tops?"

"Iss det any off your affair?" said Grandpa, giving an extra strong toss to his shovel.

---

*Dorothy's grandfather was Carl Anton Anderson; Andrew was his nickname.

"It certainly is," said Papa. "It's my boy who drinks that cow's milk, ain't it?"

"I din't ask him to drink it," answered Grandpa imperturbably, his eyes very bright above his red cheeks.

"I know you didn't," said Papa. "Don't make such foolish remarks, Andrew. You know what I'm talking about."

Grandpa leaned on the shovel and looked up at Papa. "So now you're calling me a fool," he said. "It's not enough you criticize de vay I feed my lifestock, you haf to call me a fool. Herman, *you* are de fool."

"How so?" my father asked sternly, his eyebrows coming down.

"Becauss you don't tink about dat old saying: Beggars can't be choossers. It's not my fault you bring children into de vorld and haf no place to keep dem; it's not my fault you haf to eat vot iss in my cupboard. I only offer you vot I haf—you can take it or not. But you haf no right to stand around and tell me vot to do and vot not to do."

"I *do* have a right!" said Papa, his eyes glittering and his face reddening. "If it's those turnip tops that make my boy howl all night, then I have a right to know about it, and to *do* something about it!"

"And vot vould you do?" asked Grandpa. His voice got very soft, and a little smile came around the corners of his mouth, but his eyes weren't smiling.

"I'll see that the damn cow don't eat any more of them!" said Papa. He was very mad now—I could tell that without half trying, and I felt all excited and prickly. I wondered why he didn't hit Grandpa. He was certainly big enough for it.

"Dat cow is mine," said Grandpa. "She'll eat vot I put in her crib."

"Oh, no, she won't." Papa put his fists in his pockets so Grandpa wouldn't notice how tight they were getting.

"Ven *you* get a cow, you can feed her vot you like," said Grandpa, lifting his shovel and turning his back on Papa. "But you'll neffer haf a cow—you'll be too busy haffing children for somebody else to feed."

"Andrew, are you going to keep on giving that cow turnip tops when you know it's giving the boy colic?" asked Papa. He was care-fully ignoring Grandpa's last remark.

"I don't know dat dey gif de boy colic," said Grandpa blandly, scraping the boards of the stall with the shovel. "*You* don't know. You yust think so. And you're out here telling me how to run my affairs, ven you don't know how to run your own. Iff I vas you, Herman, I vould go into de house and keep still."

"If you persist in feeding those tops to the cow, I'll have to do something about it," said Papa. He was biting the edges of his mus-tache by now, and I knew he was trying hard to be reasonable. He knew Grandpa had him where the wool was short, and there wasn't much he could do about it.

"Vot can you do?" asked Grandpa, stopping shoveling to look up at him again. "Yust vot can you do?"

Papa looked at him for a long, long minute, and Grandpa looked right back at him. I knew by the looks of them that they both wanted to fight. Papa wanted to hit Grandpa, and I didn't blame him. Grand-pa *wanted* Papa to hit him, but I couldn't see why. Surely, if Papa ever hit him with one of his big fists, he would be feeling it for a long time after.

Finally, Papa drew a long breath. "I could do one of two things," he said. "I could either give you what you deserve—a good poke in the nose—or get out of your house."

"Vich do you intend to do?" asked Grandpa, and his voice was so smooth it was hateful.

"I should do both," said Papa, his eyes glittering under his eye-brows. "And it's not because I'm a coward that I don't do what I'd like to; don't forget that, Andrew. But I think it's the better policy to get out of your house." Papa had a lot of fine words and phrases when the occasion demanded it, and he was absolutely splendid on this occa-sion. "It's just come to my mind that perhaps you had a reason for feeding that cow those turnip tops. And if I'm right, I'd be perfectly justified in not only giving you a poke in the nose, but also blacking

both your eyes. Any man that could deliberately make a child suffer
has absolutely no conscience, no feeling—"

"Herman," Grandpa interrupted silkily, "you like to use de vords.
Vords—dey are easy to use. De breath goes in, de breath goes out.
Dere's no vork to it. But vot are vords? Dey cannot put food in de
mout' nor clothes on de back nor a roof over de head. It iss only vork
can do dat. Me, I'm not so good vit vords." (This was rank hypocrisy;
Grandpa could talk anyone down.) "Me, I only vork."

"And you think I don't work?" said Papa hotly. He was getting
mad again. "I work, and you know it."

"Vid yust de hands, not de head," said Grandpa. "A man who
vorks vid bot' don't haf to get under anoder man's roof, eat anoder
man's bread—"

"Damn you!" cried Papa. "You offer me something when I'm in
a hard place, and then you make things so disagreeable I want to throw
it in your face!"

"But you *don't* trow it, do you, Herman?" Grandpa asked, and
that soft, hateful note was in his voice again. Small as I was, I knew
he enjoyed making Papa squirm, and I hated him for that. I wanted
Papa to poke him in the nose. It would have been a very good thing for
Grandpa—it might help, the way a spanking made me good.

"Yes, I throw it!" said Papa, and he was speaking very quickly,
and his eyes were like blue ice. "But I wish that if you'd wanted me to
leave you'd have asked me, without taking this way to do it. You could
have spoken like a man—you needn't have made a baby suffer."

"I vish you vouldn't insist on dat," said Grandpa, pretending to
be pained. "You do not know for sure about de turnip tops."

"But I know I'm getting out of your house as soon as I can find
another place to go!" said Papa.

"And vill you not t'ank me for de vile you haf been here?" asked
Grandpa, smiling.

"*Thank* you? Huh!" Papa snorted. "You don't need thanks. You
need—"

"I know, I know," said Grandpa. "And vy don't you do it?"

"Because any man that invites a blow the way you're doing has something up his sleeve, and the way I'm fixed now, I can't afford to let my curiosity run away with me." He paused for a moment and then added, "I can't move today, Andrew, but I will move—very soon. And from now on my boy will drink canned milk—so you don't need to worry about losing any more sleep."

He turned to leave the barn, and then he saw me standing just inside the door. He didn't say a word, just took me by the hand; I had to hustle to keep up with his long steps as he went to the house.

"Why didn't you hit him, Papa?" I asked eagerly.

"Because he wanted me to," he said.

"But he wants us to move, and you're going to do *that*—"

He frowned at me. His head was very tall against the brilliant blue of the autumn sky, and I will always remember the gulls circling in that sky, the autumn smells in the air, and the sound of the surf in the harbor—and of Papa's voice.

"You don't understand, child. Your grandfather is a very strange man. His thoughts are not like mine. He sees things in an entirely different light." Oh, those lovely, rich phrases that Papa could summon at will! Even then, while I was still mad at Grandpa, I was admiring Papa's vocabulary. "Now, don't ask me any more questions. I have to think about what I'm going to do next."

"We're going to move," I reminded him helpfully.

"That's right. I don't know where or how, but we're going to move."

We moved in a few weeks. Papa found a couple of rooms in a house nearby, down much closer to the wharf and the shore. We were so crowded that my sister and I had to sleep in the kitchen, but we were under our own roof, and there was no more crying in the middle of the night. When we met Grandpa in the road he was very polite; he bowed and smiled, and even raised his hat.

I thought how funny it was that all on account of turnip tops we had moved into a place of our own where it was nice to be—even though we were crowded—because sleeping in the kitchen could be very interesting to a seven-year-old.

In the kitchen, you were never shut away from all that was going on, no matter how early you had to go to bed. Two-year-old Ruth slept like a flaxen-haired doll on her side of the bed, against the wall, and was not the annoyance she could be in the daytime. You could lie there and listen to the teakettle singing after the light was turned low and watch the hands of the old clock move around over the numbers when you woke up in the middle of the night. And before the wood fire went out you could listen to the snap and crackle of the wood and watch the flame dancing on the ceiling through the cracked top of the stove. It was much better than living like ordinary people and going to bed in a room away from all the activity.

In fact, after a while I forgave Grandpa for being so horrid to Papa and making us move out of the little house. Otherwise maybe we'd have stayed there until Papa found a whole big house to put us in, and I'd never have known what it was like to sleep in the kitchen, where the pulse of everything we did kept up its beating. My childhood memories then would be lacking in a certain savor that I'm very glad they have.

Aunt Mamie and Uncle Joe ∾

One pleasant memory of sleeping in the kitchen concerns "Aunt" Mamie and "Uncle" Joe Alves. They used to tramp through the snow to our house night after night in the wintertime, and while Aunt Mamie snored with unrepressed gusto in Papa's Morris chair at the end of the stove, Uncle Joe and Papa sat by the kitchen table, shuffling, cutting, and dealing out the battered deck of cards, playing game after game of cribbage.

Mama would take these opportunities to get out for an evening call. It was never very entertaining for her to listen to Aunt Mamie snore, and she cared nothing at all for card games. I didn't blame her for that. The shuffling of cards, the cryptic numbers that didn't make sense to us non-initiates, the monosyllabic grunts, could all be very boring. Nobody thought Mama was a poor hostess for leaving Aunt Mamie snoring in the Morris chair while the men played cards. They knew she'd been in the house all day with small children around her feet, and going out for the evening was a good change for her.

She'd dress up warm and pull on Papa's boots, and set off toward Grandma's or Aunt Ellen's. If the night was dark, she carried a lantern; if there was moonlight, she needed nothing to guide her, for the tramped paths would be almost as plain as in the daytime. But she always needed warm mittens and a muffler. The wind that raked the little island went through to the bones, and there was no lee to take the bite of it, especially on the way to Aunt Ellen's. You had to round the curve of the harbor beach, where the surf would be pounding on the shore, a thunder in the dark, a boiling white fury in the moonlight. The wind could batter at you viciously, making the water stream from your eyes and stopping your breath, so that when you eventually arrived at Aunt Ellen's door and came into the warm kitchen, your face felt stiff and aching and you could not talk for several minutes.

But I guess Mama figured it was worth it.

Aunt Mamie and Uncle Joe were both Portuguese, but it was Uncle Joe who spoke with an accent, and it was so heavy I could hardly understand his words. He and Aunt Mamie always spoke to each other in their own language, and I used to wonder what they could be saying. I could tell by their facial expressions and the tones in their speech whether they were angry or happy or just simply content. He always called her, "Mah-ree-ah!"—just like that—no matter what mood he was in. She called him, "Mee-vay," but I suppose in Portuguese it wouldn't be spelled like that, any more than "Maria" would be spelled "Mah-ree-ah."

She was a big woman—a great, blowsy, dark-haired, dark-skinned woman, forever uncorseted—and a great one to go calling on the neighbors after her husband had gone to haul in the morning. She would get up at four o'clock, when he did, and have her housework all done by six, and then she was likely to appear in the kitchens of the neighborhood. She stopped at each home long enough to swap the daily items of gossip—always garnering some special tidbit to carry along to the next place—and share a cup of coffee and some cake or doughnuts or whatever else might be on the table. Then she would move on. She would have her calling all done by the time Uncle Joe was back on the mooring, and then while he worked in his workshop at the back of the house during the day, she baked or washed or did whatever task needed immediate attention. On summer evenings they went to bed early so they could get up early. But in the wintertime, when storms kept the fishermen from going to haul every day and the short daylight hours made the evenings too long, they came trudging to our house.

Papa and Uncle Joe must have played hundreds of games of cribbage while I lay on my bed in the dark corner of the kitchen and watched them, listening until the quiet monotony of their playing put me to sleep.

Uncle Joe was not quite so tall as Aunt Mamie, and he was much older. His hair was very gray and so was his big drooping mustache. His skin was dark and weathered to a deep brownish-copper, like an Indian's skin. He had high, broad cheekbones like an Indian's, too. He was a quick-tempered man, and when the game went against him, he would mutter and say all kinds of things to the cards, but when he was winning he would keep laughing, and scrape his thumb over the table with an odd vibrating sound.

When the cards were going against him, he was also more conscious of his wife's snoring, and he would shout at her and poke her ungently with his foot. She would be sprawled out in the Morris chair with her legs, clad in old rubber boots that were Joe's cast-offs, stretched out in the middle of the floor. She would never take off her coat, which was big enough to have made a tent for us to play in, but she would unbutton it and let it lie open. The stocking cap that covered her dark bun of hair would be standing up on her head, enough so that she was almost free of it, yet no one could actually say she'd taken it off. When Joe would shout something in Portuguese at her, she would shrug and mumble, but when he kicked her with his foot, she would open her eyes and glare at him and say something back. If he woke her up too many times, she would rattle off a long string of words in such a manner that I thought she must be calling him every bad name she could think of. I would listen with great admiration and excitement. Such a command of language would be a great thing for me, in my daily crises in the schoolyard. This was the high part of my evening. I struggled to stay awake for it.

The first time Uncle Joe would wake her up, she would merely look at him in a disgusted sort of way, repeat one particular phrase as if to say, "Oh, go chase yourself!" and fall asleep again. I thought this phrase had a very lovely sound, just the way I thought *tomte gubbe,* the way Grandma said it, was something to keep repeating to yourself for a long time after you heard it. But at the same time, I knew what *tomte gubbe* meant. They were old men no bigger than your thumb, who lived solely in the Scandinavian countries, and were great hands at souring milk and addling eggs. Grandma made us think she had seen the little men herself, because she seemed to know so well how they were dressed and the kind of shoes they wore.

Aunt Mamie's phrase was a different one. Although I whispered it after she tossed it off at Uncle Joe, I never said it aloud. It wouldn't have been any good to throw at the others when we were in a tangle, because it didn't sound bad enough. It wasn't until I was grown up that I found out what it meant, and then I was glad I had never said it aloud, because I would have been ashamed. But even today I can still admire the reckless nonchalance with which Aunt Mamie put Uncle Joe in his place. I wonder what she could have said to him when she was really in a fury. It must have been scorching.

Sometimes Uncle Joe would answer her back, and then Papa would have to butt in to calm them down and get Uncle Joe back to his game again, which he would do with much muttering and glaring from under his eyebrows.

I would lie there and laugh to myself, and then the kitchen would be quiet again, except for the kettle singing on the stove, the snapping and cracking of the spruce wood in the fire, the slap of the cards on the table, and the soft snoring of Aunt Mamie, which after a few minutes would begin to get louder.

About nine o'clock, Mama would come home, red-cheeked and

puffing but bright-eyed and in good spirits. She would make some tea and get out turnovers or cookies and maybe some frosted cake. I would lie still and listen to them talking and watch them eating (and feel very hungry). I'd also hear some important tidbit about the neighbors that I wasn't supposed to hear. Ruth would curl up behind me, next to the wall, sleeping heavily. She would waken sometimes when Aunt Mamie and Uncle Joe rose to really great heights in their words to each other, but as soon as they had quieted she would fall asleep again.

After the lunch was eaten, Uncle Joe and Aunt Mamie would get ready to go home. If it was a dark night, Joe would light up his lantern. He'd pull on his heavy reefer coat and his cap with the earflaps, drag on his thick mittens, and be ready to start. Aunt Mamie would be ready to go long before he was, having nothing to do but pull her stocking cap down over her ears, button her coat, and stomp over to the door.

With many goodnights and complimentary remarks about the refreshments, they would leave, and before he buttoned the back door for the night, Papa would call out, "Come again, Joe and Mamie. It was a good evening."

If Joe had won, he would reply heartily and say, sure, he would come again. But if he had lost, he would make some unintelligible reply, and Papa would close the door and come back into the kitchen laughing.

Not long after that, he and Mama would be in bed and the house would become very quiet. After a little while I would hear them snoring in the next room, and when I was sure I would not be heard, I would creep out of bed and go to the pantry where Mama had put away the leftovers from the lunch she had recently set on the table.

Nothing ever tasted quite so good as the piece of cake or the cookies or the turnover that I munched quietly in the shadows of the pantry while the last embers of the fire burned down to warm gray ashes in the stove. Even the crumbs of frosting were picked up by my searching fingers, there in the dark.

And when I got back into bed beside Ruth I would lie there and think of Uncle Joe and Aunt Mamie going home through the snow, the wind tearing at them, the surf smashing up against the shore near their little house. And I knew they would be making as much noise as the wind and the sea, almost, because they always argued on their way home. They never had to worry about people knowing what they said, because nobody could understand Portuguese. Without Papa there to calm them down they could say things to each other as long as they had breath. In the winter nights there was no one to hear them, and the wind and the smashing sea didn't care about them.

I was grown up when I heard the story behind their marriage, and it seemed strangely romantic to me, much more romantic than Joe and Mamie themselves. Joe and a friend of his came over from Portugal and settled in Truro, on Cape Cod. When the friend married, Joe stood up with him, and when the couple's first baby was born, a girl, Joe asked his friend to save her for him. And so his friend promised his daughter to him, and though Joe went away, he came back to claim his bride when she was old enough to be married. The bride, of course, was Mamie. It was strange to imagine her as a young girl, stranger still to imagine she'd ever been a baby at all. When I think of her snoring in Papa's Morris chair, with the stocking cap pushed up on her head and the cast-off boots sprawled out before her, and remember the beautiful and shameful insult she used to cast at Uncle Joe with such a casual air, the story seems to be about two other people.

When Uncle Joe and Aunt Mamie left the island for good and went far off to Massachusetts, to Truro, they both cried and cried. But Uncle Joe was quite an old man, and he was getting to the place where he thought he should stop lobstering. I was still a child when they went away, but the memory of them is vivid, and is especially strong when I take down my own cribbage board and deal the cards across its dark and shining surface.

The Ribbon Candy ∿

Criehaven's way of celebrating Christmas Eve was a good one. At one time, festivities were held in the little white schoolhouse overlooking Seal Cove, where the surf pounded in on the beach below while the handful of children performed in the warm, lamplit little room, speaking pieces and singing carols. Then Santa Claus—usually my Uncle Peter—came in jingling some sleigh bells and took the gifts off the big tree to pass them around. Every family was present at these occasions, and the little schoolhouse would be full almost to bursting.

But by the time I was eight, there was another place where the Christmas Eve celebration could be held. The men and women of the island had chipped in and worked together to make a clubhouse—a low, spacious building with a dance floor, a kitchen and dressing room winged on one side, and a billiard room on the other. A big piazza went along the front, and it was really a building to be proud of. Surely nobody could feel as if they were being squeezed as they sat decorously in the folding chairs watching their youngsters perform.

One tree had been sufficient to fill the little schoolhouse with the sight and scent of Christmas, but there must be two for the club-house—one on each side of the big front door. The fragrance of the big twin spruces, and the shimmer and gleam of their tinsel and bright globes and loops of strung popcorn, made them a heart-shaking delight for any child to behold.

Of course our family was very much in evidence at the "time," starched and polished within an inch of our lives. My hair was skinned back and braided so tightly that I could hardly blink, and Donald and Ruth, their fair hair shining and their blue eyes blazing, looked like Christmas tree angels. When Papa herded us all into the big room, with people standing around talking and laughing and the other children sliding and pushing each other over the big shining floor, I forgot to act as nonchalant and bored as I'd intended. I followed meekly to the place where Papa sat us down. He didn't go away to talk with any of the other men when he had us placed, but sat by Mama and held Oram on his lap. Whoever wanted to talk with us came to where we were and sat down for a little chat.

I sat still, not because I was obedient but because I was too nervous and excited to venture boldly. Ruth was too little to wander, but Donald—always the curious one—soon sidled away from Papa's knee, and in a little while he was playing with the other children and having as fine a time as any. Donald always had a fine time. He was gay mischief personified.

When everyone had arrived, the schoolteacher got us all lined up for our performance. The hour that it took for us to say our verses and sing the traditional songs seemed endless, but we got through it with a minimum of giggling and stumbling, and then Santa came rioting in, laughing "Ho-ho-ho!" in the required fashion. We could almost believe it was Santa, really, even though we knew it was only Uncle Peter. But the false beard and the red suit stuffed out with pillows made such a good disguise, it was only when you looked at the dark-skinned, tough-palmed hands that you knew it was not Santa at all.

After the presents were distributed, Santa said good night and Merry Christmas, and went out the front door with a wave of his hand, and after a while Uncle Peter came in through the poolroom door and was very much surprised to see all the presents that had been given out.

As soon as the chairs could be folded up and put away, a big man brought out his fiddle and began to tune it up. He was Papa's brother Alfred, and he could look as fierce with his mustache and eyebrows as Papa could, only he had a voice to go with them. We children were always very polite when we spoke to him. The schoolteacher played the piano, and when they struck up the music, people began to dance. They waltzed dreamily, and then they stamped and swung and swirled through "March and Circle" and "Lady of the Lake." It was a joy to watch them. They laughed and shouted to each other, and the young men lifted their partners off their feet when they swung them, and when the dance was over they panted and wiped their faces with their handkerchiefs and kept on laughing and talking.

Papa and Mama didn't stay to see the dance through to the end, and in a little while we crammed and laced and buttoned ourselves into our heavy clothes, took our presents and bags of candy, and went home. We left the glory of the Christmas trees, the warm yellow light, the music, the dancing feet, and the laughter, to face the walk home in the cold night, with the wind from the harbor blowing icily into our faces. But we brought our own noise and laughter with us, and the baby slept through it all, his head bobbing against Papa's shoulder. It was almost as exciting as the party itself, to get home and look at the presents all over again, and compare, and probably gloat. It was a good hour before Papa had us all in bed. He let us take some of our presents to bed with us, so we could look at them early in the morning—we didn't hang stockings after the clubhouse parties, since Santa Claus couldn't be expected to come twice. The bags of candy and popcorn Papa took away and put in a drawer of the bureau in his and Mama's bedroom, which was the only other room we had besides the big kitchen. Donald slept in a crib near the foot of their bed, and the baby slept in a cradle on Papa's side of the bed so he could reach out in the night and check that his littlest boy was covered and warm.

~ ~ ~

The next day we played with our new toys, and Papa gave us some—but not much—of the candy, cautioning us that it wasn't too good to eat too much of it at once. But we didn't mind that, as Mama had baked a big rooster and made stuffing and gravy, and there were lots of mashed potato and turnip and bright red cranberry sauce (made from cranberries I'd helped to pick, myself).

After dinner, everybody quieted down for a nap. It was a cold and windy day outside, with surf whipping up the harbor, and nobody was going to work. With so much good food in us, we all felt sleepy enough to agree with Papa about a nap.

All except Donald. He was always so active, so eager to enjoy every minute of living, that he hated naps. If he could have gotten out of the house undiscovered, he would have gone exploring in spite of his brief four years. He was always running away, with the twin imps of curiosity and mischief shining in his blue eyes, and I was always being sent to find him. This resulted in a constant state of trepidation for me: I never knew whether I would find him, or whether I'd get him home safely once found. He was fascinated by the shore and the boats, and once he climbed down over the side of the wharf at low tide and got into a boat. When I found him, he had no idea of how to climb up the wharf again, and I couldn't explain. Clucking as desperately as any hen who'd mothered a duckling, I rushed to one of the fish houses and got one of the men to come and rescue Donald for me. Doubtless they were all used to the sight of a round, pigtailed seven-year-old in a continual dither of breathless agitation, trying to get Donald home before he Got Into Something.

But he'd usually Got Into It before I reached him, and then he would be so cheerfully stubborn and unrepentant, so merry about the whole thing, that I'd feel as if I'd been sent to keep the tide from coming in or the wind from blowing.

On this Christmas day there was no way for him to get out of the house, but while everybody slept the heavy sleep of the just and well fed, he got out of his crib and went exploring in the bureau where Papa had put the candy. He couldn't have been hungry, but the idea must have been amusing, and the candy so gaily colored... And it was candy, and unguarded, and nobody knew what he was doing... so he ate and ate of the striped ribbon candy. I can imagine him, a little blond elf, chuckling silently while he ate and Papa and Mama slept. It was quite a joke.

No one knew about the joke for a day or so. It was only when he began to complain of a pain in his stomach that Papa began looking around to see what had made it. Papa always wanted to know what we'd been eating, and finally Donald confessed about the candy. He had eaten practically all the candy in the drawer.

The stomachache didn't respond to home remedies, and it became evident that someone must go for the doctor. Going across twenty-five miles of open sea in the winter was an ordeal in those days. The lobstering boats were small and open, the engines low-powered. The men must dress heavily, in oilclothes, sou'westers, and rubber boots, and have good tough skins to stand the stinging spray. But no matter how foreboding the sky or how rough the sea, there was always some hardy soul to go for the doctor.

The doctors had to be courageous too, and they always were. They climbed aboard the little boats and held on somehow against the choppy sea, the miles of whitecaps reaching to the horizon where the island lay hidden by the mists of spray. They took the chance that a violent attack of seasickness might lay them low.

The doctor who came to see Donald was dressed in a big fur coat, and as he was a very tall man, he looked huge to me. He had a bag filled with little bottles, and he spoke very softly, and everybody stood around and was ready to obey his smallest word. He stayed with us several days, and Ruth and I were sent up to Grandpa's house to be out of the way. Ruth was younger than Donald, and just as active, and my days were very busy. At night we came back to the house and slept in our bed in the corner of the kitchen and this took away some of the strangeness of those days. But not all, because the doctor was part of the strangeness, and he sat in the opposite corner of the kitchen, sleeping in Papa's big chair when he was not in the bedroom bending over Donald's crib.

Papa's face was drawn and lined, and Mama looked strained. As for Donald, I didn't get to see him, and I used to wonder how they could keep him in his crib now, when they'd never been able to before. It was queer to hear him crying. I didn't see him until one mailboat-day, when the doctor said Donald would have to go to the hospital. He had appendicitis, and it could wait no longer. I saw Donald then, when they got him ready to go. His face looked pointed and white, but the familiar deviltry was dancing in the blue eyes under the yellow bangs.

Papa and the doctor took him to Rockland, and I guess we all thought the operation would take care of everything. We waited for the time when we would know for sure. There was no telephone then that would have let us learn right away, and when the mailboat came there was no letter. But because there was no news at all, we thought everything was all right.

Finally, and quite unexpectedly, the word came. I can't remember how. I only knew that suddenly Mama was getting ready to go to Rockland. There was much hurrying around to get things together in a small trunk, and I heard talk that my Aunt Ellen, Uncle Peter's wife, would come to the house and stay with Ruth and the baby and me until Papa came. Still I heard no word about Donald. But there was a strange, set look to people's faces, and Mama was crying when she thought nobody was looking.

When she got ready to go to the boat and start for the mainland, we children were told to stay home and be good until our aunt came to be with us. I remember sitting by the window with Oram in my lap and Ruth kneeling on a chair with her small face pressed against the pane while we watched Mama go down to the wharf. One of her brothers carried her trunk to the boat. We could see everything, almost: the people going in and out of the post office on the wharf and stopping to talk with their heads bent and their faces sober. You'd hardly think they were the same ones who'd whirled and stamped, laughing, through "Lady of the Lake" not a week before. We could see the surge of white on the harbor ledges, glittering under the winter sunlight, and the gulls flying, and the skiffs and dories bobbing on the bright, blue-green water. It was a gay, shining, blustery day, but no one looked gay. It was a day when ordinarily I'd be out—with Donald, maybe chasing after him to keep him out of mischief. But instead, Donald wasn't here, and we others were alone in the kitchen that seemed oddly empty with both Mama and Papa out of it. The fire crackled with unnatural loudness in the stove, and the clock's ticking was tremendous. Ruth and Oram must have felt the strangeness too, because they were so quiet.

Yes, we could see everything from that window. We saw my uncles and some other men carrying a big box up from the wharf to Grandpa's house. Ruth said, "What's that?" But I couldn't tell her. I couldn't guess what it was.

After a little while my aunt came, and she took me to one side and told me that Donald had died, and I was to be quiet and not make any trouble, and to help her all I could with the other children. I didn't believe her, but I was too polite to say so. I had a feeling everybody had been fooled, somehow, and only I knew the truth.

When I went up to Grandpa's house, I was not allowed in the sitting room, but I saw other people going in, and coming out with tears in their eyes. For some reason—my disbelief, I suppose—I didn't ask to go in to the sitting room, or worry about what might be in there. I had no bad dreams; there were no unpleasant shadows around Donald's name for me. It was as if he had simply disappeared. He might never run down to the shore and the boats again—never on Criehaven—but as for being dead, that was something else entirely. That wasn't Donald. He'd always hated to take naps.

I hadn't known, while we were looking out the window to watch Mama go down to the boat, that Papa had come home that day after all. He had seen Mama at the wharf, and had spoken with her, but then he had been so overcome with grief that he had gone off to his workshop and stayed until it was dark, so that no one could see him or speak to him. Then he came home, and my aunt went away. I could not feel sad about Donald, but I know I grieved for Papa. A terrible quiet hung over us. My sister and I could not keep our eyes off Papa, who stood in front of the window for a long time, or sat slumped in his chair with his hands over his eyes. It seemed as if his head, which had always been so proud and high, would never be proud and high again. It hurt me to look at his face, but I could not look away from it. The light that always seemed to be with him was gone. There was no laughter in his eyes, and when he spoke, his voice held a sadness that spread out from him until it hung over everything—the house, the island, the ocean to its outermost rim.

The next day Donald was buried. We children did not see any of the ceremony. We just kept very quiet and ate what we were given and did as we were told, and when people looked at us they had an expression that was new to us. It was sympathy.

Two weeks went by, endlessly, and then one day when the mailboat came, it brought something else for my uncles to carry to my grandfather's house. But still Mama didn't come back, and still no one told me anything. That afternoon I went up to Grandpa's, hoping that someone would tell me something without my asking—the feeling that still hung over the family was forbidding to a child. My youngest, favorite uncle, Charlie, who was not much older than a boy at the time, asked me if I didn't want to see something in the sitting room. I followed him curiously, not dreaming what I would see.

In a little casket, there lay a tiny baby, dressed in a lovely, long dress. It was exactly like a doll with its closed eyes, its little hands doubled into fists. He asked me if I wanted to touch it, and I put my forefinger gently on one of the tiny fists. It was very cold. I looked up at my uncle with questions in my eyes, questions I didn't know how to ask, and he said quietly, "This is why your mother isn't coming home for a while. She doesn't feel very good. She went off to have a baby. This is the baby, but it was born dead."

I looked at the baby. It didn't make me feel like crying, but it made me feel strange. I felt that if I stared at it long enough it would open its eyes, the little fists would uncurl, the small pursed mouth would stretch in a yawn. It would be alive, and then Mama would come home.

"Is it a boy or a girl?" I asked.

"A boy," he said.

"What's his name?" I asked.

"He hasn't any name."

I looked again. It was my brother, but he had no name. Didn't he even have a last name, I wondered. But I didn't ask.

Then my uncle took me out of the room and closed the door, and when there was another funeral, neither Ruth nor I knew any more about it than we'd known about Donald's.

Finally Mama came back, and there was a heavy sadness over our house for a long time. Where there should have been three boys there was only one, and the house had a dark, empty feeling. There were tears in Mama's eyes most of the time; in Papa's eyes there was a deep brooding, and harsh lines in his thin face. His arms, which were always ready to hold his children, now seemed to want to hold Oram the most. I could understand why: Oram was a boy, the only boy he had left.

I heard Papa talking with Mama one day, and they mentioned the ribbon candy we'd gotten at Christmas time—a night that now seemed so far away, and clouded by all the sorrow that had come since.

"It was that candy that made him sick," said Papa. "If he hadn't filled himself up with that candy, he'd be alive now." Papa's face tightened up and became drawn and stern; his lips were pressed so closely together they made a thin pale line across his face. "Don't ever let me see a piece of that kind of candy in this house again," he said with a softness I couldn't forget, because it was like the softness that goes with the deepest sort of rage—or grief.

And whenever Christmas came again, and we got bags of candy and popcorn, he always took the ribbon candy and threw it in the stove. And when he shut the lid, he dropped it with a crash.

The New
Playhouse ~

As soon as spring came, with all the budding of leaves, the breaking forth of the first strawberry blossoms, and the warm rain muddying the roads into rich, dark stuff perfect for mudpies—as soon as all this began to happen, the children of the island began to collect things for their playhouses. We were as assiduous as the birds who had just come up from the south, and much more unscrupulous. It took a great deal of scheming to get to certain trash piles, always full of treasure, before one of our cousins did. Spring was a stimulating season in more ways than one.

Behind our house, the spruce woods grew thick and near, and in their shadow there was many a nook that was perfect for a playhouse. It fell to my lot, since I was the oldest and the strongest, to get the boxes and boards for cupboards and dressers, and this also called for a crafty strategy. When I had collected enough, by my own nefarious methods, I nailed the boxes to tree trunks in the chosen spot, laid the boards across a rock or a couple of projecting tree roots, and there was the dresser. Ruth took care of the dishes, making cakes and pies and puddings with frenzied abandon, while I wandered through the woods looking for fern roots—little horn-shaped delicacies, creamy white, and possessing a nutty sweetness. I collected these in Prince Albert tobacco tins, and we called them bananas. Then there were the tender, pale green spruce tips, and whatever lumps of spruce gum that I could pry off the bark. This would keep us champing energetically for hours. If I happened to be near the shore, where the waves might be either washing with a gentle whispering sound against the jumble of rocks or making a great thunder and bursting into tremendous explosions of spray, I would follow the waterline like the solitary sandpiper. There might be some bits of wood that would make new furniture in the playhouse. If I found a strayed pot-buoy or bottle, or a trap that had washed ashore, I carried them to the grass-ground above high-water mark and then told Papa about it later so he could bring them home.

The way my sister and I kept house was the way all the island children did. Each family had a playhouse, and there was always one or two from the group who looked for fern roots and gum in the woods and watched for things to drift in from the far-flung sea. We never had a sense of the island's minuteness. To us it was our home, and if it rose rock-rimmed from the sea and was forever besieged by the waves, we felt no humbleness, but a rather startling sense of our own importance: We lived on an island. The smaller the island was, the greater our stature. The sea was no enemy, but a part of our domain, and we accepted it casually, as we accepted the sky. But we could not breathe away from it. It was our universe.

Sometimes our playhouse would be near the house, and sometimes we'd have it so far from our back yard that it would take us fifteen minutes to get to it—Ruth and I and the younger children down to the current two-year-old. But then, we never walked as a crow flies; we might stop to slide down a steep rock, or climb a tree, or turn over a stone to watch the ants run, or take a look at the trash piles in the woods behind our neighbors' houses.

Those trash heaps were like books to be read. You could find out what people took for medicine, whether they used Epsom salts for physic, or Atwood's Bitters. You knew if they drank brandy or gin—

that was a wildly exciting and sinful discovery!—and you knew when their pots and pans wore out and when a plate or cup had been recently broken. And then there was always the chance that they had bought something new and had thrown out the old utensil when there was hardly a thing the matter with it. Holes could be plugged with a bit of rag, handles weren't necessary, and if you should find something like a flour sifter that would really sift, then you were practically in the same class with people who wore silk and had an extra pair of shoes for best.

In the matter of playhouses, the competition was sharp. Our cousins visited us, and we visited back. We discussed each other's dishes, graciously or acidly as the moods went, and remarked on the merits or faults of the household arrangements. The comments sometimes reached great heights of frankness, and finally we came to blows, which brought the nearest parents into the battle.

One of our worst wars sprang, like all wars, from small beginnings. It was on account of a teakettle that I took from my cousin Helen's playhouse on an unannounced visit. We'd all suffered because of that teakettle, and Helen's superior attitude toward our playhouse indicated that you were Really Nothing unless you had a teakettle. So I simply sought out her playhouse—when she wasn't in it, of course—and took the teakettle. When next she came to visit, we told her we had a new teakettle, and we were suitably nonchalant about it. She cast a supercilious glance at it, recognized it, and broke into anguished screams. That was one of the times when we were safely out of the reach of parental interference, so I strong-armed her out of the place. Helen and I spent most of our childhood with our foreheads pushed together because we had a death-grip on each other's pigtails, so I don't know why I thought she had given up when she went home without the teakettle. I do know that, in the end, Papa was brought into it. He stood there like Solomon, confronted by a wailing Helen and a square-built, belligerent Me, and said finally, "Oh, give her the goddamn teakettle!"

It was my turn to be anguished, more by the sight of Helen's triumph than by the loss of the teakettle. I was pushed into the house, fighting every inch of the way, and forbidden to visit Helen's playhouse or to invite her into ours. But these crises arose often in the spring, and in a day or so were forgotten.

We hardly got anything from our own trash pile, because when Mama got through with anything, *nobody* could use it. When a hole appeared in the top of a kettle, Papa mended it with a rag , and the soup that was cooked in it tasted as sweet as ever. Handles could come off and still the cup could be used. The only thing that Mama would throw away would be a broken cup or plate, and we never bothered to take them to our playhouse. The neighbors, however, threw away things that were merely nicked or chipped, and they were perfection compared to the china that Mama threw out.

Our playhouses were wonderful things, and when I consider them now, I marvel at the imagination we displayed. Invisible walls were as strong as lath and plaster—we went through a door only where the door was indicated—and if one of our cousins came to call and stepped through a wall instead of the door, as was polite and necessary, it was almost cause for a fight. And if a cousin wanted to be insulting, he persisted in walking through the side of the house and being very stupid when you showed him his mistake.

I used to tire of the commonplace games, and would turn a playhouse into a blockhouse in a state of siege, or a castle with a moat around it, or a homesteader's claim, or a ship on the rolling deep. On those occasions, Ruth was always in the kitchen or galley while I defended us against Indians or wolves, or steered our ship safely to port.

If we could tease Mama into giving us some biscuits and molasses and a quart jar of water to take with us when we went to play, then it was a special day; we had real food to eat, and didn't have to go through silly motions over a cracked dish full of mud sprinkled with green spruce spills for frosting.

Through the spring and summer we moved around in the woods and along the back shore like gypsies, shifting our playhouse when the mood struck us. By fall the way of our moving could be traced by the abandoned bits of broken china and tin cans and bottles for which we had no more use.

One day—a day that has become a historical milestone in my memory—Papa began to build a new outhouse. The old one was a rickety affair, with a door so small that Papa had to stoop very low in order to enter. I was always drawn irresistibly by the sounds of saw and hammer, so I stayed around to watch, and discovered that this new outhouse was going to be tall enough for Papa and wide enough so that no one need ever feel crowded.

All the children gathered each day to watch Papa saw boards and nail them into place, and it was generally agreed that he was erecting a fine building. Its boards were bright and new, and it stood in the shelter of a tall spruce whose great low-spreading branches gave it a nice sense of privacy, which was of course desirable.

When the building was done, we were proud of it and proud of Papa for being able to construct such a sensible and practical thing. Papa was proud of it himself. While he was working on it, he would stand off and look at it and purse up his mouth and squint his eyes, and then fill his old corncob pipe and puff away as he walked around examining his fine job.

Everybody knew what he was doing, not only because the children went to their respective homes to relate what was going on but because the sound of his hammering and sawing echoed far across the village and the harbor on those blue-and-crystal summer days. Whoever looked to see where the sound came from could see the new building rising in the shadow of the giant spruce at the edge of the woods.

We gazed at it with new pride every time we walked toward it. Mama gave us some old calendar pictures to put up on the walls inside. We knew we had something that the rest of the neighbors didn't have—a brand new privy. We had moved up a notch on the island's social scale.

During the lovely, soft summer days when the Closed Time was on and nobody had any traps out, Papa used to go fishing for cod, which he salted and dried for our winter's use. It was on one of those days, when the sea was the same forget-me-not blue as the sky and the distant mainland lay in gentle lavender curves along the luminous horizon, that Ruth and I were suddenly visited by the same idea. We were tired of our playhouse as it was. We had wanderlust. We wanted to change our street number, and what could be better than the new outhouse? We trudged back and forth through the woods with boxes of dishes and bottles and rusty tin cans until we had all our household goods assembled in front of the outhouse. Then I took some of the boards that had been left over from the construction job and laid them side by side over the seat for a beautiful new, clean dresser. I took our box cupboards, which had been nailed up and taken down so many times, and nailed them against the walls. My sister got busy putting away the dishes—kettles in a box that stood on its end in the corner, cups and plates in a cupboard on the wall. The old frying pan that had only two holes in it she placed at the end of the dresser, and the shiny bottles she stood along the back of the dresser, against the wall.

At last we stood off and admired, as Papa had stood to admire his work. We had a real playhouse at last, a place where the rain didn't come down to make puddles in the middle of the floor, a place that had real walls and a real floor, so no insulting cousin could say, "What wall? I don't see any wall." There were real walls for them to touch, a genuine door that would close behind them—or in front of them, if they got too uppity. The door had a hook on the inside so you could hold off Indians for as long as you had food and water, and there was a small window at the side where I could stand and watch icy seas rolling over the fo'c'sle.

We played all afternoon, and nobody came to bother us. Mama had taken Oram and gone to visit Grandma, and she would not come home until she saw Papa come into the harbor to pick up his mooring. So the hours slid by and nothing marred our perfect enjoyment.

We were deeply engrossed in an argument as to who was going to the store for sugar (to the beach to get a pail of fine white sand) when we heard someone trying to open the door, and then we heard Papa say, "Hurry up in there! There's other people who'd like to use this place, you know!"

Ruth and I gazed at each other, open-mouthed, too stunned to speak. Then we looked at our array of dishes. Everything in place. Everything so spic-and-span. The whole arrangement so elegant after the playhouses in the woods. And now we would have to disarrange everything.

But maybe not everything. Quickly we took the bottles and frying pan off the dresser, stood the new boards against the wall, and went outside, blinking innocently at Papa. We said nothing when he went in. Then we heard him say explosively, "For the love of Mike! What do you kids think you're doing—making a playhouse of this toilet?"

We made no answer, but stood around and waited until he came out. He glared at us from under his terrifying brows and said, "You'd better take that trash out of there! Hurry now! That's no playhouse!"

He went off down the path to the house. We went inside and stood looking at our things, and our hands were too heavy when it came to carrying anything outside. Instead, we put the boards back for the dresser and placed everything as it was before.

By and by Mama came, and again we took off the boards and dishes and went outside to wait. She said the same things that Papa did, with even more emphasis, and went back to the house. We returned and put things back the way we'd had them.

It came to be suppertime, and Mama called us to eat, and we went merrily to the house. After supper was eaten and the dishes washed, Ruth and I were sent to bed. We whispered long about our new playhouse and talked about what we should do the next day. In an indirect way we would contrive to arouse our cousins' curiosity, so they'd come to call. And *then* wouldn't they look foolish! This would pay Helen back for making such a fuss about her old teakettle.

We fell asleep when we were tired of watching Papa sitting in his chair reading, and Mama mending some stockings under the lamp. We fell asleep still thinking about our playhouse.

Suddenly we came awake. Papa was standing in the middle of the kitchen floor, talking very loudly to Mama. It was about our playhouse. We lay still and listened.

"My God, Agnes," he said. "What will those kids think of next? Where do you think they have their playhouse?"

"They had it in the toilet, last I knew," she said. "But I told them to clear out."

"Well, I told them to move it, but they didn't! And when I went in just a few minutes ago, I didn't know what kind of stuff I'd run into!" Papa's eyes flashed, his mustache seemed to quiver. "I set plumb down on a mess of mudpies, and it give me quite a start! I fished out a match and lit it—and, my gosh, I bet they got enough junk in there to fit up *ten* playhouses!"

At this point I could restrain myself no longer. "What did you do with our things?" I cried, rising up in bed.

He turned and looked at me. "Nothing much. But I want all that stuff cleared out of there in the morning, or I *will* do something. You mind that, now. And don't forget."

"No, sir," I said dolefully, and settled back in bed.

The next morning Ruth and I sadly dismantled our beautiful home and went slowly back to the woods that had sheltered us all through the spring. We had many playhouses afterward, going from one place to another as our fancies dictated, but somehow we were never able to forget our brief day of glory.

The Lobster Smack ~

O ne of my most pleasant memories concerns the two-masted schooner *Conqueror*. In my childish imagination, her black hull and towering masts made her a mysterious and beautiful ship as she came out of the west, from Boston, her sails curved and billowing in the wind and snowy as the foam on the sea. We children could see her on the horizon if we happened to be playing on the western shore of the island, and it was always our delight to watch her come closer, growing steadily larger, until she was in full view, the water breaking away from her black bows and rippling astern. We loved watching her come into our tiny harbor, where she loomed big and high, and we would follow her by land as she made her way in. We stood gazing with entranced eyes as she took up a mooring and waited for the men to come in from hauling. She never took aboard lobsters when she came from the west, for then she was on her way Down East and her reason for coming into the harbor was to unload the freight she had on board for the fishermen and their families.

Nearly every man would order something for the captain to bring on his return trip. I can remember that Papa always ordered boxes of milk crackers, kegs of salt pork, barrels of sugar, molasses, and flour, besides the twine and rope that he needed for his traps. You could get the captain to buy a big barrel of cookies—broken, but good—from Cobb, Bates, and Yerxa. That was a fantastic and outlandish name, but then, anything that was away from Criehaven was outlandish to us. We could not visualize or even imagine any other world but the little island where we lived. It was small—no more than three hundred and sixty-five acres—and very rocky, rising abruptly from the sea, but it was big enough for children who found its shores and woods exciting and wonderful.

When the captain of the *Conqueror* had unloaded the freight, he would get under way again to collect lobsters Down East—another mysterious territory that had its reality only in the stories Papa told us. On his way back to Boston, the captain would stop with us and collect what lobsters the island fishermen had saved for him. The *Conqueror* was about the best-lined schooner I had ever seen, and I thought she was the most beautiful ship in the world. I had seen sloops; there were a great number in the harbor at Matinicus, the next island, and they were constantly moving about the islands, near and far. To me they were commonplace. Grandpa had a small sloop, but most of the boats in our harbor were small, with neither mast nor cabin. Nonetheless, in those small boats the men went much farther and worked harder than some of the fishermen now, who have bigger boats and better and faster engines.

Watching the *Conqueror* come with such a gallant air from beyond a horizon that seemed the veritable edge of the world was more thrilling than watching a plane arrive at the island today. She brought good things as well as money for lobsters. She also had mystery, for she had nudged strange wharves and her canvas had slatted and filled in the air of ports that were only names to us. And beautiful as any plane might be, flying like a gull across the sky, it could never hold a candle to the beauty of the *Conqueror* as she came with her sails curved in a dazzle of white, her black sides glistening in the sunlight. I didn't know it then, but I know now that she was poetry; I hadn't yet read John Masefield, who wrote of sails and spars. I was only a sea-bred islander who had never seen the mainland and gave little thought to its existence until I saw a new vessel, or a stranger—or the *Conqueror.*

I thought that to be the captain of such a schooner must be the most wonderful life a person could lead. I imagined living on board the *Conqueror,* and although I had never seen the inside of the captain's cabin, I knew that it must be a snug place. I knew positively that to stand on her deck, looking up at her sails and masts, with my hand on her big wheel, was the most satisfying feeling in the world.

But the sad fact was always being borne in on me—with the help of a multitude of relations—that I was a little girl, and there were Some Things little girls did not do, Some Things toward which I might not aspire. It had begun when Papa's mother took away my clay pipe and my broken jackknife, and it had been happening ever since. I knew that I could not hope to own a ship like the *Conqueror* and be her captain, guiding her through calm and storm, so I must content myself with dreaming—but not with *sitting* and dreaming. I turned tall trees into masts where I could climb and look for sails in the far distance. I turned rocky shelves on the wildly rugged western shore into broad decks where I felt the salt spray on my face. On rainy days, when I had to stay in the house with the other children and amuse them while Mama visited Grandma, I managed to turn our kitchen into a cabin and the other children into mates, cooks, and seamen. If the rain beat hard against the windows, that was good, because it meant that we were bucking a stormy sea and having hard weather of it.

I did more than steer an imaginary wheel while I stared grimly out the window at an imaginary ocean in the throes of a typhoon; I worked my sister Ruth into being cook, and there was nothing too good in the house for us to use for our meals. Mama had tablecloths that she never put on the table for ordinary wear. She had a chocolate set and a beautiful glass wine decanter with glasses to match. The chocolate cups were small and delicate, and the wineglasses were tiny, with slender stems. They were doll-like, and they tempted us irresistibly. They seemed meant for us. Never mind that Mama had impressed upon us many times that we should *never* touch them; they were wedding presents, and cherished. But who could explain to her that when she left us to tend the fire and keep the kettle boiling, her big kitchen magically changed, and her flock of children changed too? How could we have made her understand that when one had an extraordinary ship to steer, nothing but extraordinary things could be used aboard that ship?

So out would come the tablecloth when the captain decided it was time to go below for a meal. And who could stand in the captain's way when he decided that ordinary cups and glasses were too plain for him and his crew? Who wanted to argue, anyway? The other children enjoyed drinking from the tiny, fragile things. The warm water and milk, with a bit of strong tea for flavoring, never had a sweeter taste than when it was drunk from those precious cups and glasses.

But we had a good many rough voyages. One by one the dishes were broken. We felt unhappy, of course. Unhappy in more ways than one, since we knew what was in store for us when Mama discovered what we were doing with her treasures. Luckily, she kept the sets on the top shelf in a dark pantry, supposedly safe from us, and it was a long time before she missed them. It was too late then to do much about their loss; they couldn't be replaced.

Papa's best trousers were blue serge, and they always hung in the closet in his room with the suspenders all attached. We liked to dress up when we played, if it was possible, and while the others took what they wanted from the closet—Mama would have paled to see what happened to her good dresses—I always claimed Papa's best pants, by right of some sort of eminent domain, being the captain and the biggest.

Papa was over six feet, and I couldn't have been more than four feet tall; therefore, to keep the legs from dragging, I had to roll them up. I must have been a ridiculous figure, but fortunately the younger ones didn't think so, and I was able to command the respect I wanted. Captain Bligh had nothing on me. The only trouble I had with them was when the lookout, who was posted at a window, sang out as Mama hove into view across the fields. I had to move fast to get out of my pants and keep the others moving too, to get the tablecloth put away and the forbidden dishes tucked back onto the top shelf. Sometimes it would be a close call, and Mama would be on the doorstep by the time I had shed the trousers. I wouldn't have time to hang them in the closet, so I'd roll them up and chuck them under her bed and wait for a chance to retrieve them and put them back where they belonged.

Mama and Papa never could understand why Mama's dresses so often had their sleeves wrong-side-out or why Papa's pants didn't keep their press very well and had mysterious kitten-tails of dust on them, since he wore them only on Sundays and always was very careful with them.

We also could never explain what happened to the beautiful white woolen blanket that Papa won when he bought a ticket for a raffle. It was a wide double blanket, soft as down, white as snow, and Papa was very proud of winning it. But it was much too beautiful to use every day, so it was put away with the nice tablecloths and doilies that Mama didn't want messed up by her careless brood.

We couldn't tell Papa that one day I figured that the kitchen was too big for a cabin, and that we should partition it off. We brought out the blanket and found that it would reach across the kitchen, corner-wise. And of course when we fastened it, we couldn't just tack it lightly with a couple of nails. I had to use about fifteen nails, and drive them in deep. I loved using a hammer, and the woodwork was just right to take nails, with a great deal of solid satisfaction on my part.

We had a wonderful time dodging in and out of the blanket. It was amazing what a difference it made to have two small rooms instead of one large one. I can remember looking at the blanket partition with complacent pride. It was really just the thing. No matter how violently we went under it, going from one side to the other, it was securely fastened, and on shipboard that was the way things were supposed to be.

But when the lookout yelled, "I see Mama comin'!" there was no time to pry at the nails with the hammer or the butcher knife. We had to move things fast and get them out of sight. It took quite a bit of frantic tugging to rip the edge of the blanket loose from the wood-work, but at last it came, and triumphantly I replaced it in the pantry, not thinking much about the odd, ragged, scalloped effect along two sides of it. When Mama came in, she found us quiet and well be-haved, more than willing to take the wheelbarrow and some grain bags and go pick up chips from the beach so she could make a quick, hot fire for biscuits.

At a much later date, Papa had occasion to ask Mama to bring out the blanket so he could show it to a caller. He was very proud as he opened it up and let them feel its texture. I was there, watching in unusual silence—for me—but he never looked in my direction when he discovered the distinctly unique notched sides. He looked at it keenly, so did Mama and the visitor, and they shook their heads in amaze-ment. Nobody could imagine what the notches were or how they came to be there. It wasn't until after the caller had gone that Papa looked at Mama, as he puffed thoughtfully on his corncob pipe, and said, "I have an idea about that blanket. There was a reason why it was raffled. There was something in the making of that blanket that was-n't right. That's why it was raffled off. Nobody could have ever sold that blanket right out. It would have been cheating."

Mama thought about it, and it sounded right to her, so she nod-ded. Nobody looked at me, and I was glad. I was glad, too, that I'd had presence of mind enough to dig the nails out of the woodwork before they were observed, although Papa did remark once that he had never before noticed that line of gouges on the door casing, and how did Mama suppose they got there? But Mama didn't know, and when we were asked we didn't know either.

"I swear, it's funny how you can go around not noticing," Papa remarked. "Those gouges were probably there when we moved in, but we just didn't see them."

After that, the blanket was taken out to use every day, because Papa decided it wasn't a first-rate article, so it wouldn't do any harm to get some good out of it.

New Babies! ~

I was ten years old when Evelyn was born in 1915. She came along in May, a year and a half after the little boy who'd never opened his eyes to life. She was round and fat and rosy, and always cheerful from the very first. Now there were four children and two adults living in two rooms. Ruth and I still slept in the big kitchen, where we could watch everything going on until we fell asleep. In the other room, Mama and Papa shared a big, wide bed. It had to be long enough for Papa to stretch out in and wide enough for Mama to be comfortable when she was almost ready to have a baby. At the end of the bed stood the white iron crib in which Donald had slept. Now Oram had it, and the wooden cradle at the side of the bed was for Evelyn.

Ruth, Oram, and I came down with measles the next summer, and we had no sooner recovered than Mama and Evelyn were sick. Papa had his hands full until the siege was over, and in the fall of 1916 Oram came down with infantile paralysis. Two other children on the island also got polio, and the doctor came out and stayed, and again there was a dreadful cloud over our house. The shadows under our parents' eyes were deep. Were they going to lose this boy too?

The atmosphere was tense for days, but Oram pulled through.

Except for the fact that he couldn't use his legs, he was once more his happy-go-lucky, merry self. For a long while he crept around the floor as Evelyn did, but gradually he began to stand on his feet, and then he was once more running and skipping with his usual vigor. He was always a skinny, wiry little creature, and it wasn't until he was around twelve that one shoulder seemed noticeably lower than the other and he walked with a slight swing to one foot. By the time he was turning twenty, it was almost forgotten that he'd had the dread disease. It was only when one cast back into the past for a date and said, "Oh, it was that year that Oram got infantile," that it was remembered.

Back in those years Papa was doing well. He was able to make money lobstering, to pay bills, to have new babies coming into his house. His boat was small, a sixteen-foot dory partially decked over, with a small engine. Besides lobstering, he went handlining and raised a pig, chickens, and a garden. He'd been raised on a farm, so it was natural for him to have good luck with his vegetables and livestock. And because he was able to raise so much food, he wasn't forced to go to the store for everything, so his bills kept diminishing. Then another baby came along [in 1917], and things really seemed to be looking up for Papa. This baby was a boy, and Papa had not only him, but money in the bank: two hundred dollars. It was a rich sensation for us children, something else to lift us several notches on the measure of social and business success.

Papa was able to rent another room in the house, so now we had three big rooms on the ground floor. We really felt spacious after being cramped in two, except that going to bed early lost all its charm completely when Ruth and I were moved to the sitting room to sleep. It was very dull to be shut away in there. We weren't allowed to have a lamp, and we couldn't hear what was being said out in the kitchen.

It was while Mama was on the mainland having her new baby that Papa came down with a sickness. He'd have spells when he lay on the kitchen couch looking gaunt and white and helpless, though he never complained. We children would walk lightly and keep out of the way, but we weren't worried. He had always had terrible headaches—migraine, I suppose—and we were used to that.

One day in November, when the sky was gray with sparsely drifting snowflakes and a grim, cold wind tumbled a gunmetal sea into whitecaps, I walked home early from school to start dinner. While Mama was away, the teacher would let me off half an hour early, and if Papa hadn't yet come back from hauling his traps, I'd build up a fire and heat water. Ruth and Oram and I would have some fried eggs or fish hash or warmed-over chowder for our dinner and then go back to school. Evelyn was with Mama on the mainland. At night Papa would always get our supper.

On this day I knew Papa wouldn't be hauling. I thought he was perhaps in his fish house building traps. When I came to the shed door and saw the kitchen door had blown open and a tiny triangle of snow had drifted across the sill, I was not disturbed. But when I came into the room and saw Papa lying half on the couch and half on the floor, and looking as if he were dead, my heart and body went into a panic. All I could do was to turn and run as fast as my short legs would take me, around the harbor to Aunt Ellen's house. I remember that it was like running in a nightmare. The wind seemed to press me back, and though my legs pounded wildly on the frozen earth and then on the plank walk laid over the beach rocks, and I could hear the pounding, still it was a lifetime before I stumbled up Aunt Ellen's steps and through the summer kitchen.

I don't know how she could understand what I said, because my throat ached bitterly from my running against the wind with my mouth open, and because for the first time in my life I was struck with the terror of death. When my brothers had died, it had seemed like a strange sort of disappearance; Donald simply wasn't there anymore, and the little baby had never lived with us, so he hardly seemed to belong. But the sight of Papa's face, so gaunt and seamed and ashen, and the way he lay on the couch as if he'd lost consciousness before he could get his whole length on the bed, had an impact that I couldn't miss. Now I *knew*; now I had come face to face with the full reality of it. And I knew, all the time I was running that nightmare race to get Aunt Ellen, that I could not live without Papa. He had always been two-thirds of my universe; now he was all of it.

Aunt Ellen was a big woman, brisk and unsentimental. Whenever she came into a house where sickness was, everyone felt better immediately. The sick person was relieved by the sound of her voice, by her very manner of walking. The family, in that moment, became a little less worried.

Somehow she understood me, calmed me with a crisp, "Now, now—," got into her coat, and went home with me. But this time I wasn't less afraid, because I was sure of what she would find when she got there. Sure that this time she would look at Papa and then shake her head. When we came into the kitchen, I stood in a sort of paralysis as I watched her go to him and touch him. He was on his side, and I could see where blood had come from his mouth and soaked the couch covers. As I looked, my stomach turned sick and my head felt dizzy and strange.

But he wasn't dead. When Aunt Ellen touched him, his eyes opened. She lifted his legs and put them on the couch and spoke to him. Then she turned to me.

"Build the fire," she said. Her voice was the way it always was, brisk and unworried. "Be quick about it, now!"

My hands were trembling, but I built that fire in record time, and set the teakettle over the blaze. As I worked, I could hear Aunt Ellen talking to Papa, and knew he was going to try to clean up and get dressed in his best clothes and go to the mainland, where a doctor could do something for him. The mailboat was due at any moment, and would stay just long enough to put off the mail and freight.

Papa went into the bedroom, and in a little while he came out wearing his blue suit and his black overcoat—an overcoat that always seemed very choice and luxurious to me, since it had a narrow velvet collar. When he wore that coat and his felt hat, he looked not at all like a fisherman. With his lean face and his erect, soldierly carriage, his eyes so clear a blue under his heavy eyebrows, he seemed very handsome to me in spite of his illness. And frightened as I had been, I could look at him now with the warm sparkle of pride that I always felt about Papa. A few moments ago I had been sure he was dead, and I'd faced a world, a lifetime, that had gone suddenly bleak and lonely as the November day around me. But now he was alive, and able to walk, and he was dressed in his black overcoat—surely he would come back from the mainland all well and would never be so horribly sick again.

I made tea and took a big cup of it to him; he drank it, scalding as it was. Then he asked Aunt Ellen to stay with us while he was gone. He walked down to the wharf, in the teeth of the north wind and the cutting snowflakes, and I watched him as I had watched Mama go down to the wharf the day Papa brought Donald home. But it was different now, for Mama had been trying not to cry that day. Today, just as he left the house, Ruth and Oram arrived home from school, staring at him in admiration and astonishment, and he managed to smile at us and tell us that he would see Mama and report that we were all behaving as well as she could ask.

Once the small gasoline launch that carried the mail had left the harbor with her nose in a smother of spray, we felt that Papa was as good as cured, and we began to feel a steadily rising tide of excitement. Aunt Ellen was going to stay with us. She was jolly and full of funny stories, and she never objected to entertaining small fry like us. Though she'd been born in Gloucester, as Mama had, she could tell us tales that Grandma and Grandpa had told her of the old country. She could even say words in Swedish, which to me is still a fascinating, lilting tongue.

Life took on a colorful tinge. We went back to school filled with our own importance. It was no commonplace thing to have one's father make a sudden trip to the doctor and to have a jolly aunt sleep in your house and get your suppers for you. We made quite a story of it to the teacher and the other children.

I settled down to my books, glancing occasionally out at the whirling snowflakes that by now made a shimmering white veil between the schoolhouse and the harbor. The wind whistled around the corners of the small white schoolhouse, and I wondered how it must be to cross the bay. I could picture the heaving, surging expanse of dark water, the whitecaps hissing as the wind sped them along; I could see Papa smoking his corncob and talking to the captain. But I could not imagine him landing at the wharf or going up the street, or whatever he would do after he arrived at the mainland. It was as if he must go on and on across the water and disappear into a mist of whirling snow. What lay beyond was a complete mystery. Rockland was twenty-five miles away, and it was as legendary a port as Boston. Two things alone were certain: He would go to the doctor—the one who had come when Donald was sick and again when Oram was sick—and find out why he had fainted and bled from the mouth, and he would see Mama and talk to her, and tell her we were behaving well.

He came back in two days, with medicine to take and instructions to be careful about his food. He had stomach ulcers, the doctor said, and what had happened to him that snowy day was a hemorrhage. My picture of his trip was entirely wrong. I heard him telling Aunt Ellen how he'd had another hemorrhage and had lain in a half-stupor all the way. It had been terribly rough; the little boat was hardly fit for such a trip, and there was no place for him to get under cover. The spray had blown in on him when the boat smashed into the rushing waves. There were six or seven full bags of grain in the cockpit, and he had managed to lie on these, wondering in his conscious moments whether the boat would ever reach her port. He said he had been a proper mess when he landed. There was blood on his nice coat, and it was covered with dust from the grain.

But anyway, he said, he did get there, and he was feeling a lot better, and he'd seen Mama—and guess what? We guessed quickly. It made no strain on our imaginations: a new baby. Papa's eyes were bright as water with the sun on it when he nodded.

"A boy," he said, quietly enough, but I sensed his joy.

"What's his name?" Oram clamored excitedly.

"Russell," he said. "Russell Linwood."

It was a beautiful name. It sounded as rich as the black overcoat with the velvet collar. We said it over to ourselves and each other. I was not as gratified about a new baby as I should have been, perhaps—I was the one who had to wheel the baby carriage over rough island paths during long afternoons that could have been spent more profitably as far as I was concerned. But still, the name helped. It was impressive.

We went back to school with renewed importance, and since the teacher and the other children were suitably astonished and respectful, we settled down to our lessons with a flourish, a certain debonair nonchalance. We might not be like other people on the island, who had a whole house to themselves, but we had a new baby rather often, and nobody else could lay claim to anything like that!

Chores ～

My twelfth year was a banner year. It was then that I made my first trip across the bay and saw the mainland rising out of the sea—first in little scraps of spruce-grown islands, and then big ones, and then mountains against the sky. They were as purple as the Concord grapes I had seen sometimes, and as the mailboat slipped in under the shadow of Owls Head Light, the mountains became blue and then a smoky green. Below them, the lower hills smoothed out and became fields that came down to the water's edge. For the first time I saw Owls Head Light and the Rockland breakwater, and looked up the bay toward Camden and Belfast. For the first time I saw cobblestones and electric cars, and ate ice cream that was not homemade, and even went to a photographer and had my picture taken.

That was also the year I tried to be a Campfire Girl. The Jameson girls and their mother, our only summer folks, arrived that year full of Campfire lore, and determined to Make Something of me. Any suspicions of Mama's that it was an organization devoted to frivolity were dispelled by Lorea's careful explanations. I would soon display an unusual interest in dishes, sewing, cleaning, etc., since I would win beads for all my achievements. It would be the best thing in the world for me. She talked seriously with both my parents, and Papa, who was used to enduring a battle royal between Mama and me over the smallest household task, decided it would be a good thing for me.

I was skeptical. But they had asked the other island girls to join, and Mama even signified her willingness to run up a vaguely Indian affair of brown cambric for my uniform. I was supplied the wherewithal to make my own headband, but the beads and other equipment had a habit of disappearing. (Our house was crowded, and the younger children were exploratory.)

I really tried to be a Campfire Girl. My headband turned out to be a wide black velvet ribbon, which, when bound across my brow in the approved manner, broadened my Scandinavian face to Neanderthal proportions. The fringe of my dress brushed the tops of my shoes, and on meeting days I smuggled my outfit across the village and over the island to the Jameson cottage, because my contemporaries who were *not* Campfire Girls were frankly and richly expressive about my get-up.

The struggle was an uneven one. For a little while our family enjoyed the unusually harmonious relationship that existed between me and my parents. But soon the painful battle to win honor beads for sewing and housework was too much for me. I was no good with a needle. I, who loved to swing a hatchet and who could pry out nails with a murderously sharp butcher knife, quailed when I had to pick up a needle. Housework had long been used for punishing misdemeanors, and I couldn't force myself to do it now for a little colored wooden bead.

After a while the leader grew suspicious when I "forgot," week after week, what I had done to win beads during the past week. She tried, gently but firmly, to lead me out of my devious ways. But dirty dishes remained dirty dishes, and I would as soon face the sword of Damocles as a needle. I was not at all a credit to the organization. What prompted my final departure from the ceremonial fire was the imminent arrival of my cousin Helen. I knew that if she joined, I couldn't stand it. Helen *liked* to sew; Helen liked everything I didn't. Much more fragile in appearance than I, she nonetheless was adept at housework. I pictured myself writhing inwardly while Helen reported on her weekly progress to an admiring circle. I pictured our walk home after the meeting, sneering at each other, with Helen indisputably in the right. It would be like the time when Papa made me give the teakettle back.

I left the Campfire Girls. Papa was disappointed, but somehow he too had never really believed that it would work.

Having tasted of independence, I next announced that I was done with wheeling baby carriages. I had decided that since there would always be a new baby in the house, and since it was one of my chores to wheel the baby along the paths when the weather was fine and warm, I would be wheeling baby carriages for a long time to come unless I made a stand now. Mama was quite sharp with me, but I stood firm. Whether she thought my attitude might be disastrous for both carriage and passenger, I don't know, but at last the job of wheeling the baby was given over to Ruth.

There was more time for me to gather wood if I didn't have to wheel the baby, so after school and on Saturdays it was the usual thing for me to take a washtub on the wheelbarrow and trudge along the paths till I came to a beach. Out of the tide-washed rockweed I picked up chips and small pieces of wood until I had the tub filled. Longer pieces I would lay across the handles of the barrow, and Papa would chop them to stove size when I got back to the house.

It was never any real task to pick wood. I could take my time about it, and there was something very entrancing about the beaches, where the tide was always coming or going. The dark spruce woods rose up mysteriously behind me, filled with an unearthly silence in the late fall and birdsong in the spring and summer.

There was always a chance of finding an interesting bit of wreckage, buoys, bottles, or pretty shells. There was the beauty of the sky, whether cloudy or clear, and the colorful, ever-changing sea, whether calm or dancing in a light breeze, or racing and tumbling in a gale. The rocky shore, with its sharp crags and slanting shelves of rock, was awash in color—warm tan, tawny pink, dark brown, volcanic black, granite gray glinting with bits of mica or quartz. On the pebbled beaches I'd find treasures of driftwood, perhaps a gull walking at the edge of the water or a flight of sandpipers. And everything was mine, mine to see and smell and embrace.

I learned the shape and size of the island, and all the nooks and crannies of the shores when I searched for wood. When the time came that I could take Papa's dory to the farthest end of the island, with Ruth and Oram and Russell and Evelyn aboard, picking wood was a real adventure. It was a delight to row along the high, rock-walled shores and land on the beaches that made deep scallops between arms of rock. It was exciting to put the dory's bow on the pebbles without bumping, in a good clean run, so that she slid high enough above the tide for you to step ashore without wetting your feet. It was fun for us to scatter quickly along the beach and fill the dory as soon as possible. If one beach had but little wood to give us, we would go on to the next.

Getting back to the harbor was always an occasion for joyful pride on our part. With the dory loaded high and the children perched precariously atop the load—scarcely daring to breathe, since they knew what would happen if one of them moved suddenly—we came home, wanting everyone to see how Herman's children saved him both money and labor. We felt sure we were giving Papa reason to be proud of us. The hardest part of the whole business was to get the wood from the dory to the back yard. We'd throw it all out onto the beach just below our house and then use the wheelbarrow and our shoulders to carry it to the chopping block. And then, if Papa didn't have time to fit it for the stove, we wielded the axe and saw until the entire load was ready for use. We worked. We tugged and grunted and puffed. But when Papa came home from hauling and looked at the woodpile, then glanced around at us from under his eyebrows, and finally smiled and said, "You've done a good job," we all felt warmed and refreshed and not tired at all.

There were times when he wouldn't allow us to start out in the dory. Even when there wasn't a breath of wind there could be a heavy undertow. But often, when he'd gone to haul, and the sun was warm and the sky clear and the ocean silkenly blue, we'd take the dory off her mooring and take a chance on finding a safe place to land in spite of the undertow. I hesitate to think what might have happened to us if the others hadn't been so well behaved, so prompt to obey when I gave the word. But they were a good crew, and they knew enough to respect the deep, cold waters that surrounded our island home. They might have been a handful when we were ashore, but in the dory it was another thing.

We respected the sea but we were never afraid, and while the gulls soared over us and the crows scolded us from the treetops, and the inquisitive seals bobbed their shining heads above water to see what we were doing, and the wild black ducks, the sea-pigeons, the loons and the sheldrakes, flew away as we approached, we were having fun and working at the same time. And we were absorbing without knowing it some of the vast wild beauty that surrounded our childhood.

Our imaginations were always busy on those trips. This might be a desert island. An undiscovered foreign country might own these wooded shores. At other times we simply went back into the past, when the Indians owned the island and there was not a house in existence—we'd wiped them all out—and right around the next point we would see tepees and canoes and feathered topknots.

Matinicus Rock Light was always a romantic sight. It was a turreted castle—a castle with a moat, a castle with battlements. When it was stormy, the tiny rocky island with its towers was a giant battleship, always sailing proudly into the east or west. (It all depended on the wind.) And although she always stood still, in our imaginations she was constantly moving, plowing the raging sea, tossing the foam high into the air.

Matinicus Rock stood three miles away from us, with a foghorn that talked to us in thick weather and two lights that glowed like mysterious and watchful eyes at night. Years later, the twin lights were changed to a single one that revolved. By that time, we'd had the chance to go and see the place for ourselves. We saw the houses and engine house and boat house and towers, and learned how they stood close to one another and so formed in the distance the illusion of a castle or a super-dreadnought.

Even today, Matinicus Rock rides arrogantly against the horizon for me, and I see it still as something mysterious and majestic and unchangeable. So will it always be for island children.

Our island consisted of a flat, cleared lowland between two high, wooded ends that ran off into long, rocky points. The Western End was barren and uninhabited, rich with wild strawberries in summer and possessing a desolate beauty in winter. At the Eastern End, Papa's brother Fred owned a small farm, cut off from the rest of the island by a thick belt of spruce woods. The central flatland was narrow and indented deeply by the harbor and three coves. The very narrowest part was flooded by the ocean whenever a severe storm and an unusually high tide came simultaneously. These fields produced most of the hay that was cut on the island.

Most of the village grew up around the harbor, but at the eastern edge of the flatland, against the dense spruce woods that separated it from the Eastern End, the Rhodes farm sprawled spaciously across the island from one shore to the other, and from the woods to the harbor. Fred Rhodes had married the only daughter of Robert Crie, who had settled the island in true pioneer fashion in 1849 and had given it its name. The Crie homestead stood on a rise, apart from the rest of the settlement, where it could look across to the Rhodes place or down to the harbor and beyond to Matinicus and Vinalhaven.

The Rhodes farm was called Hillside, and with the spruce-banked hill rising above the dwellings, and the big barn with its silo, the place seemed appropriately named. We bought our milk from there, and it was one of my chores to trudge the wide road with a tin pail and bring home the daily quart.

I went after supper. It was one time of day when I wasn't herding along a flock of small children, but at the same time, I was somewhat afraid of the dark, having a certain knowledge that ghosts lived in the cemetery a little distance from the Crie Homestead and that the glowing eyes of Matinicus Rock Light could watch me almost all the way. The only thing I could do to keep the ghosts from rising above the trees and wavering through the night was to whistle loudly and strongly and continually, and anyone could trace my journey by just listening. It was one of my life's trials that Mama had a horror of my whistling and firmly believed in the old saying, "Whistling girls and crowing hens always come to some bad end." I received many slaps and reprimands for whistling, but I couldn't stop, and because I was ashamed of being scared of the dark, I couldn't tell her why whistling was so important.

It wasn't so bad going after the milk as coming back with it. Going over, the cemetery was behind me and I could keep my head turned rigidly away from the unblinking eyes of the Rock Light. But on my way home, even though I still kept my head turned away from the Light, I was facing the cemetery and the dark, gloomy woods that enclosed it. So I developed the habit of sitting in the Rhodes's kitchen with silent persistence, trying to put off the moment when I would have to take my pail of milk and start home.

Ignoring all hints about departure, I'd sit and sit, with a certain stolidity that must have been maddening to the kindly Rhodes family. As the evening wore on, various members of the family would suggest that my mother would be worried, and wasn't nine o'clock my bedtime? I would assure them, heartily, that nobody ever worried about me, and I never had a special bedtime, anyway.

Even as I explained this, with artful candor, I knew that I'd have a lot of explaining to do at home, too...of a rather different sort. But I never could make Mama understand. When she asked me, with a determined glint in her eye, where I'd been and why I'd stayed so long, I would stare back at her mutely or say that I stayed because I wanted to. I wouldn't admit that I was scared of goblins—of which Grandpa told me much—and ghosts, and the eerie gaze of the Rock Light.

Sometimes Papa would come after me, and I'd be ashamed to have people know he was cross. I was also ashamed to let him think I was being a nuisance to other people, but it was a relief, and worth being ashamed, to know he was stalking along ahead of me through the salty island night. He said nothing, but puffed away on his corncob, and the scent of it was perfume to me. Even if I had to hurry to keep up with him, and arrived home puffing like the corncob, I was glad. With Papa near, no ghosts dared lift their white floating bodies above the trees and come soaring down upon me, and the eyes of the Rock Light lost their penetrating brilliance and became two round lanterns that made shimmering tracks on the dark water between the islands.

The Rhodes family was always having visitors, interesting people from the mainland—and not only from the local mainland, but from all corners of the world. Ministers, artists, musicians, teachers— all summer long Mrs. Rhodes, stately and white-haired and gentle of voice, presided at a full and cosmopolitan table. The visitors were all fascinated by Criehaven, and I was fascinated by them. The time I spent in the Rhodes's kitchen was never dull. The new faces, the strange accents, the fragments of conversation that I caught, were like something from another world. And when one of these visitors took it upon himself to walk home with me, I was pleased and flattered. He simply took his hat and said he was taking a walk to the harbor, and if I was ready to go home I could walk with him. That was all I needed, just to know I wouldn't have to whistle constantly as I hurried along the rutted road. It was pretty hard to whistle and hurry. My mouth would get dry and I'd be out of breath, and the dread of losing my pucker at any moment was as bad as the dread of the ghosts—who, of course, would unfailingly know the instant I stopped whistling.

To be escorted home with the milk became the usual thing. The visitor's name was H. Latimer Brown. He was thin and fairly tall and sandy-haired, with a drooping mustache. He was an artist who worked in watercolor and pastels, and he wore a corduroy jacket with big pockets that carried pads and pencils and boxes of what I called chalk.

When he went walking in the daytime, he sometimes carried his easel and his watercolor box and a little stool, and during that summer he sketched me many times. I didn't see any of the pictures but two, since he didn't like to show what he was doing. One of them showed me helping Papa haul up the dory—Papa so long and rangy in his old clothes and rubber boots, and myself short and square-built. The other sketch was of me alone, sitting on the edge of the wharf fishing. My back had been toward him when he made the drawing, and I was very much ashamed when I saw it. My dress had lost most of its buttons, and when I leaned forward to watch my line, it had become very evident that I should have been at home, busy with needle and thread, instead of dreaming in the sun over a fish line. There, on paper, was the shameful proof of what Mama kept saying: I should be Learning How to Be a Lady. I asked him, red-faced, to destroy the picture, but he said he couldn't do that—it was one of his best. I couldn't see anything "best" about a pigtailed girl fishing off a wharf, with her face not showing, and there, for all the world to see, the evidence that she was careless about her buttons.

The last night Mr. Brown walked home with me was sad because I knew he would be leaving on the mailboat the next day. He said that he didn't know when he would come back. Perhaps he would never come back. Although he never asked questions, in fact rarely spoke to me, there was something about him that made me feel at peace. When we parted near the corner of my house and I said good night, thanking him bashfully for walking home with me, he handed me a cigar box and said in his dry way, "Maybe you'll get a little fun playing with these."

He turned and walked away. When I got into the house, I

opened the box eagerly and found that it was full of the colored chalks I'd watched him use. There was every color I could imagine. Some were broken; some were whole. Papa and Mama looked at the chalks, and I told them Mr. Brown had given them to me. Papa puffed at his pipe and looked thoughtful, and then he said, "That was nice of him."

But Mama didn't think so. She said they'd get my hands and clothes dirty, and I found that was so. I couldn't draw pictures and I had none of the coloring books that children have today, but I had a small blackboard, so I used the pastels like chalk when I played school with the other children on rainy days. (When Mama didn't go to visit Grandma, our games were necessarily reserved and circumspect.)

Of course bits of the chalk were dropped and trodden into the floor during the course of the school sessions, and the colors were hard for Mama to erase from the soft wood. One day she lost her patience and put the box and its contents into the stove, slamming down the cover with a gusty sigh of relief. She'd had about all she could stand of those messy things, she said. Now, when I look back, I hardly blame her, but then I was heartbroken. Not so much for the pastels, but because Mr. Brown had given them to me. I waited summer after summer for him to return, but he never came back.

Sunday School ∼

Because the Rhodes family had ministers visiting them so often during the summer, the island people could enjoy church services, which were held in the little white schoolhouse that stood above Seal Cove, halfway between the Rhodes farm and the fishermen's homes at the harbor. On Sunday mornings Mrs. Rhodes held Sunday School for the children, and in the evenings there would be a regular service, with a sermon preached by the minister who happened to be visiting. There was always a big turnout, as befitted the chief social event of the week. Everybody liked to sing hymns, and the ministers were always good talkers. It was somewhere to go. It was pleasant to see all your neighbors together in one room, and if it was sometimes crowded and rather warm, who cared? It made things just that much cozier.

I liked Sunday School except for one thing: I had to be nurse-maid, companion, shepherd, and sheepdog to my brothers and sisters. It was no easy job to keep the littlest ones from stubbing their toes and falling down to dirty a clean, white pair of trousers or a starched, lace-trimmed dress. Somehow I never seemed to bring them home the way they started out. It would have been unbelievable luxury to go to Sunday School alone, without being obliged to anticipate whatever the others would manage to do on the way. I would have enjoyed getting into a mood suitable for the day, catching a sense of exaltation from the bright blue sky and the far-reaching sea. But the sterner things of life kept me from slipping into any mood but a bad one, and my patience would be almost worn threadbare by the time Mrs. Rhodes called us together inside the schoolhouse.

I could have sat peacefully on the schoolhouse steps awaiting the summons, breathing the clean, sparkling air with its indefinably lovely fragrances of the sea, the wild roses that grew in myriad pink stars around the schoolhouse, and the sweetgrass in the marsh. I could have watched the seagulls soaring in their clean-cut whiteness against a sky that seemed to have a special Sunday polish on its summer blue...

All these things I could have done and seen. Instead, I spent the time seeing that Oram and Russell did not slide down the big boulder behind the schoolhouse on the seats of their brief white trousers. If one of them stood on top of the boulder and defied me, in a manner which shattered any remnants of my Sabbath mood, I had to go up and get him, which risked skinning the knees out of my white stockings. Ruth could have been expected to look after Evelyn and keep her fairly spotless while I rode herd on the boys, but unfortunately these pre-Sunday School meetings offered fine opportunities to carry on feuds that had flourished all week—and Ruth's temper was fiery. Sunday was especially good, because you could cause superb damage to your opponent's best clothes instead of his or her everyday overalls or gingham.

Exhausted, scowling darkly, and muttering un-Christian sentiments under my breath, I would welcome Mrs. Rhodes's gentle call to worship. Sensibly, she always started us off with some good rousing, cheerful hymns, and by the time we came to our lessons I would be ready to enjoy myself. The other children would be in their own classes, and for a little while I could pursue life at my own tempo. I loved to sing—we all did—but the lessons were the best. I could always think of questions to ask. Once I dared to ask how anyone could be sure that Adam and Eve were the first man and woman. This question really caused a sensation. Mrs. Rhodes, after the first shock, tried to explain. I looked dubious. She explained further and my doubt grew more obvious. I muttered that since it all happened so long ago, how could anyone be *sure?* Mrs. Rhodes countered that since the Bible told it, I should be able to accept it as truth. I wanted to know how anyone could prove the Bible was telling the truth. I knew how stories changed when they went from house to house on the island.

Finally, Mrs. Rhodes and I both gave up, momentarily out of words, and thenceforth I remained silent on the Adam and Eve story, though unconvinced. For the most part, I could accept the lessons and go on from one to the next, until there came a day when I was learning the Ten Commandments.

I was busily memorizing them in the morning while Mama was getting the others ready for Sunday School. Papa was reading a magazine and holding the baby, and things were quite peaceful, until I asked suddenly, "Papa, what's *adultery* mean?"

He looked up, startled, his eyebrows rising and then coming down thickly over his eyes. He shot a frosty blue glance at me. "Ask your mother," he said gruffly. I was surprised, because he had never failed to answer any question I asked. But I turned to Mama obediently and asked her what *adultery* meant.

Mama pressed her lips firmly together and gave Papa a peculiar look. "You tell her, Herman." She seemed disconcerted. "I don't know how to say it."

He looked back at her as if she'd failed him somehow, and then he looked at me. I waited, wondering why they were tossing the word back and forth. Why was it so difficult for them to tell me?

Finally Papa said, "Ask Mrs. Rhodes when you go to Sunday School. She'll tell you."

"But why can't *you* tell me?" I argued. I couldn't understand why they were passing the buck to Mrs. Rhodes. "If she can tell me, you can."

"It's part of your lesson, isn't it?" he said severely. "Then talk it over with her." He went back to his magazine with an air of finality. That was the end of it. I looked at Mama, who had a funny look around her eyes and mouth, and I knew that it wasn't because they were ignorant of the word that they didn't tell me. They knew, but they didn't want to say.

I went back to memorizing my lesson, but my mind wasn't on it anymore. I kept thinking of the way they'd evaded me, and wondering why. And suddenly I knew I wasn't going to ask Mrs. Rhodes. I shouldn't have to ask her; why should she explain to me something that my parents wouldn't tell me?

I went to Sunday School, and when it was my turn to give the Ten Commandments, I recited them rapidly. I slowed on the seventh, and watched Mrs. Rhodes closely, but she didn't seem to get a funny look in *her* eyes about it. She looked just the same as she did on all the other commandments, and when I'd finished, she told me in her quiet way that I had done very well. So I didn't pick up anything at Sunday School that was very informative about adultery. Almost immediately I forgot to wonder anymore.

But when school began in the fall, something must have brought it to my mind, and I asked one of the older girls what it meant. She took me over to the big, fat dictionary that lay on a desk at the back of the room, opened it up, and after a moment she pointed to the word.

"There it is," she said, without getting very excited about it. "Read it for yourself."

I leaned over and read, "Adultery. A violation of the marriage bed." I looked up at the older girl.

"Is that all there is to it?" I asked, trying to sound as casual as she looked.

She nodded and walked away. I read the definition again. It all seemed so simple, so easy—there it was in tiny black letters. "Violation of the marriage bed." But, I asked myself, what in heck was a marriage bed, and how did you violate it? I wanted to call the other girl back and ask her, but she'd thought I would understand what I read, and I didn't want to show my ignorance. If she thought I knew, then I'd make believe that I knew, but I made up my mind privately to watch out for marriage beds and see if I could detect any violations.

I knew I could not ask any more questions at home, and I was a little angry and disappointed with Papa for not telling me in simple language what the dictionary had so plainly printed. I didn't see any reason why he and Mama had tried to shove it off on Mrs. Rhodes. After all, the meaning must be simple enough—it didn't take many words for the dictionary to tell it. I didn't have the sense to look up the word *violation,* and perhaps I wouldn't have understood any better if I had.

I was haunted for years, so it seemed, by all the things a marriage bed could be. Finally I decided it was some special bed made up for people when they got married.

And because I dared not ask any questions, my ears were always pricked to hear any mention of such a bed. It seemed as if no one in my immediate vicinity—in the small world of the island—had ever had one. There were spool beds, iron beds, trundle beds, cot beds; single beds, double beds, feather beds, and four-poster beds. But no marriage beds. Nonetheless, I had seen a strange expression in Mama's eyes and a tightening of her mouth, and Papa had been too gruff in the way he'd answered me, and my school friend had been too casual in the way she'd opened the dictionary and then walked away. I was sure that there was *something* about marriage beds that was not so simple as the dictionary would have me believe.

Matters Spiritual ∾

Papa was never the one to insist that we go to church and Sunday School; it was Mama who saw to that. And Mama never had to push us to attend the little services that were held in the schoolhouse. We enjoyed the singing and the lessons, and if we didn't quite understand what the visiting minister was driving at, we still had a good time. At the evening services, the strong, deep tones of men's voices swelled through the little room in the old hymns: "Let the Lower Lights be Burning," and "Jesus Savior, Pilot Me," and the others beloved by people who lived by and from the sea. From the schoolhouse windows that looked toward the harbor we could see the dulled fires of the afterglow in the western sky and sea, and the appearance of the evening star as the twilight deepened. The kerosene lamps filled the schoolhouse with their soft glow, shedding a kind radiance over weatherworn faces and into the uplifted eyes of children. All the voices sang together, and the sweet tones of the tiny organ blended in, until to me it all became one worshipping, melodious sound.

Papa never went with us. He stayed home with the littlest children, and it was Mama who walked along the path with us. We behaved a little more decorously on the path in the evening. In the mornings, going to Sunday School, we frolicked like young animals.

If we hadn't enjoyed church, if we'd teased to keep from going, Grandpa would have been certain we were heathens in mind and soul as well as body. His religion drove him so hard that he had no patience or tolerance for anyone who read anything but the Bible. Well, maybe a newspaper was all right, to tell you what was going on in the world, but nothing else. He would turn absolutely rigid with disgust and horror when he came into our house and found Papa or any of us children reading a book or magazine. He would shake his head and mutter to himself in Swedish, and it surprised him not at all that Papa's finances were always on a lower level than most people's. The printed word, to Grandpa's mind, was used more by the devil and his followers than by the saints. Regarding me as a brand to be plucked from the burning, he collared me whenever he could and made me sit down at the dining room table with him while he read out of the Bible and told me what it meant.

It was very boring to me, but I didn't dare tell him so. I felt that I knew quite a bit about the Bible; I didn't need to listen to him droning along in his broken English. He would read for a while, then look at me suddenly and say, "Do you understand vot dat means?"

I'd nod, thinking he wouldn't follow it up, but he'd always say, "Tell me vot it means." His piercing eyes, his gruff voice, and his directness annoyed me. I knew well enough that he thought we were all heading for hell—he told me about it frequently—but I didn't think it was his place to pull us back from the yawning chasm.

Grandpa was never a gentle man, but in all fairness I must say he was generous. He would always share his food and his working tools, but although everybody enjoyed Grandma's wonderful yeast rolls and Swedish breads and the coffee she brewed so well—and ordered specially from Rockland—nobody leaped to borrow anything from Grandpa unless driven by the utmost necessity. Grandpa usually followed along to see what they did with a borrowed tool, and told them what to do and how to do it. And Grandpa never told it pleasantly. He handed out lectures with his loans, and one had to be hardpressed indeed to want to borrow so much as a small turnip.

He was a small man, a strong and energetic one. He worked hard, from long before daylight until well after dark, and he expected others to do the same. If they didn't, they were lazy, and laziness was a deadly sin that went hand in hand with ungodliness. No matter who came into his presence, man or woman or child, he could find an opening in the conversation to launch him on his favorite topic.

According to him, he had never seen such a lazy assortment of people as the ones who lived in his present neighborhood. Nobody knew how to *work*. Everybody did just enough to get by. Everybody thought of getting things done as quickly as possible and then sitting down to loaf, to read, to talk—"spinning cuffers," as he called it. Wasting time that could be put to good use.

He firmly believed that we wasted more time and were lazier than anyone else. It grieved him to think our family was really part of his family. We were his grandchildren and—worse shame—Papa was his son-in-law. Papa, who read books and smoked his pipe when there was work to be done. Papa, who liked to spin cuffers and tell of his experiences when he was a young man in the North Woods. Grandpa had had experiences too, but it was seldom he spoke of them, and then only to point out a moral. He knew what it was to reef a topsail in a storm; he knew all the brutal hardships that were the other extreme of John Masefield's glowing poem, "Sea Fever." He knew intimately the cruelty of the old-time bucko mates, and he had lived through it all because he was made of harsh, indestructible fiber. He looked upon Papa, the dreamer, with scorn.

Little that we children did escaped Grandpa's eye. He knew of Papa's leniency toward us. He saw us taking the sharp hatchet and dulling it with our amateur efforts; he saw me rowing off in the dory when I should have been at home washing dishes; he heard Mama calling to me and saw me go my own merry way, and knew that Papa would do no more than give me a sad and gentle reprimand. He would walk into our kitchen, his eyes narrow and sharp above his high, broad cheekbones, and see the books and magazines lying around—Papa and I were always borrowing them. Leveling a work-callused forefinger at them, he would say in his most cutting and ominous voice, *"Trash! Dat's all it iss—trash! Not'ing dat is good for de mind. It just teaches to sit down and do not'ing."*

I would always leap up with an eager defense of my books. I told him loudly that if you didn't read anything, you didn't know anything, and he would turn and look at me as if I were the meanest of worms that crawled the earth. "Vot you mean, *know* anyt'ing?" he would ask scornfully. "Do you read anyt'ing dere dat tells you how to vork? How to stay home and help your modder? How to sew and scrub de floor? Does it say how to cook and how to go out and vork and get yourself some money?"

"No, but it tells you how other people live and what they think about things," I'd say.

"Odder people!" He would hesitate as if he were making up his mind whether to waste time and breath on me, then burst out vehemently, "Vot you care about odder people? Vot you care how dey t'ink?" He would point his finger at me until it almost touched my nose, and it was a point of honor with me to look him in the eye and not back off. "Neffer you mind about odder people—you yust mind about yourself!"

I could not argue with him. I would be getting furious myself by then, and Mama would send me out for a pail of water or off to get some chips from the beach. I'd go eagerly enough—anything to get away from listening to Grandpa talk about the evil of books.

He never came into the house and made such talk when Papa was there. He'd tried it once, and Papa had said calmly, "Don't you like to read, Andrew?"

Grandpa puffed up importantly. *"Ja!* I like to read. But I read de *Good* Book. I read de Bible."

"Then go home and read your good book, Andrew," Papa advised him tranquilly. "Read and see if you can find anything against a man sitting down and relaxing in his own fashion after his day's work is done."

Grandpa darkened with anger. "It vould do no harm to you, Herman, if you read de Bible. Dere is much you could learn."

"I have no doubt about it, Andrew," said Papa, looking at Grandpa with a glint in his eyes. "But the Ten Commandments and the Golden Rule seem the most important to me. I know what they are, and I try to live by them, so now I can go on and read something else."

Grandpa knew it was no use to try and save Papa, so he went away. But that didn't stop him from talking to the rest of us. I asked Papa what made Grandpa the way he was. Why did he have to keep after us, making us feel that we never did anything right, that we were living in the wrong way no matter what we did or said? What did Papa think was right?

"Your grandfather has lived a hard life," Papa said. "He had to be tough to stand it. That's why he has no patience with people like us. It's a habit with him to be always working at something. He does not know what it's like to ponder over things, except to worry about the devil and hellfire. He's not interested in anything else." Papa shook his head. "He's well and strong, and he has to keep moving. He doesn't read the Bible because he's happy; he reads it because he's afraid. He's afraid of the devil and hellfire, and it's too bad for a man to live in such fear."

"Aren't *you* afraid of the devil and hellfire?" I asked, suddenly realizing that I wasn't scared, myself.

Papa looked at me soberly. "I know the Bible tells of the Judgment Day, and if we haven't done right, we'll go to hell," he said slowly. "But somehow I have a feeling that God won't judge men the way they judge themselves. He isn't going by outside appearances. He knows what's on the inside of us, and no matter how the world judges us, that's no sign God will judge us the same way." His lean, tanned face grew stern, and he pointed the stem of his pipe at me. "Now, I don't mean for you to think that I don't believe in reading the Bible—I've read a good part of it myself—but you don't have to read the Bible all the time to make you good or to make you believe in God. All you have to do is look around you, and if everything you see doesn't make you believe in God, then all the Bible-reading in the world won't do you much good either."

So it was that, many times, when I walked along the shores alone and marked the vastness of the ocean as it gleamed under the afternoon sun, I could feel the nearness of God, and I knew that was how it must be with Papa when he was out by himself, hour after hour, hauling his traps in shimmering blue calm or in crisp, boisterous northwest weather. He must have felt then how near God was to him, and there must have been a certain peace with the knowledge, a certain contentment deep and sure as the ocean itself, for he never seemed afraid to go out even in the raw windy weather, although his boat was so tiny, so old, so weak in her timbers.

It must have been with Papa the way it was with me, when my sense of the solitude of the island and the greatness of the sea would sometimes grow to such inescapable proportions that I felt smaller than the tiniest kinglet in the woods. Yet I didn't resent the feeling, for it was then that I stopped to think of what it said in the Bible about the creation of the world. Certain phrases stayed with me and repeated themselves in my mind, seemingly without volition on my part. When a shaft of sunset light broke out below the clouds and poured fiery radiance on the evening-shadowed sea, or when the sunrise colored the sky like the inside of a shell, touching the ocean lightly, paling the stars, revealing all distances, gilding the islands and the craggy islets where the gulls were waking, the same words always came to me: "And the Spirit of God moved upon the face of the waters."

They had such a holy sound, those words, such a holy meaning; and the colors in the sky and sea, the silence that lay all around, over the great distances as far as I could look, added so much to those words that I would stand in a kind of awe, hardly breathing, feeling almost as if tears were coming to my eyes. I knew then what Papa had meant when he said, "There's more to the Bible than just reading it." He should have added, "You must think about what you've read," for that must have been in his mind.

When I stole away from the house at night and took the dory off the beach, and rowed outside the mouth of the harbor, to sit there drifting with the tide, watching the trembling reflections of the stars on the calm black sea, I would think of what someone had written long ago, in Genesis, about the way God made the stars and set them in the firmament to give light upon the earth. Under the tremendous arch of deepest blue, drifting on the breathless sea, I would feel tiny and insignificant, and yet I would hold a vast and complete peace. I was not afraid. It seemed as if I had never been afraid and never would be afraid. I would drift and dream in the darkness, as secure and trusting as a gull.

The gulls in their flight gave me the same feeling about God, the same certainty that He existed. I tried to write poems about them. God and the sea and the island and the gulls were all mixed up together. The poems weren't very well written, but they gave me a lot of pleasure. They said what I felt. I suppose if I had taken one of those poems to Grandpa and let him read it, he might have thought that some of his lectures were bearing fruit. But I couldn't do it. He was so set against books and reading that I couldn't bear to take the chance that he would look at my poems with contempt.

Grandpa told me, after I was grown up, that his heart's desire had been to see me become a missionary. I was startled. I could not see myself as a missionary. He sighed after he told me, and I felt a little sorry for him. To be truthful, I felt rather sorry for me, too. A missionary's life might have taken care of the itching foot that later troubled me.

Grandpa might truly have had his heart's desire, if he'd had Papa's way of interpreting the Bible. He could have impressed me and given me an interest in the daily reading he considered so essential a part of life. And in turn, I might have wanted to teach, as he tried to do in his blunt, impatient, and highly uncomplimentary fashion.

I wish now that I could have explained to Grandpa that Papa was not leading me into the paths of unrighteousness by letting me read everything that came to my hand. Perhaps if he had understood, he would have been more tolerant of Papa's nonconformist way. He would not have looked upon him with such scorn.

To be frank, I believe that neither Papa nor Grandpa had much love for their fellow men. They had seen too much; they were too cynical. But Papa loved young things, children and animals. Grandpa had no patience with young things, except perhaps with the plants that grew in his garden and could later be eaten. Papa had an abundance of patience and pity. He could annoy me very much at times, when he tried to explain that people weren't necessarily vicious in their minds when they did ugly things. His idea was that human beings, on the whole, were a pretty poor lot, but not because they wanted to be.

My idea was something like Grandpa's, I realize now. I thought that people were downright cussed and meant it. I hated those who tormented Papa with many nasty little words and deeds during the years when we were growing up, when he was considered soft and shiftless not only by Grandpa but by others on the island. I argued hotly for revenge; if it had been left to me, I would have found innumerable ways of getting back at the ones who hectored Papa because he was not as grasping and avid as they were. But Papa wouldn't hear my inflammatory remarks. He always quenched me—on the surface, anyway—with one of the platitudes upon which he had apparently been reared: "Two wrongs don't make a right. They can't help the way they are."

"They can too!" I shouted. "They know what they're doing all right when they haul your traps day after day! The boys know what they're doing when they steal our Christmas rooster to cook with their darned old hen-taters!"

His eyes would be very sad and have a sort of tired expression as he looked at me. I'd still be talking fast and loud. "Nobody would do things to *me* and get away with it! I'd find a way to get even!"

"You know what it says in the Good Book," he'd remind me quietly. "'Vengeance is mine, saith the Lord.'"

That usually stopped me. "Well," I'd mumble, "I don't see how you can be so meek all the time, and never get sore when people steal off you and sneer."

"What they steal from me can never do them any good, and what they say can never hurt me," he answered. "You're too young to understand it now, but someday you will. If I steal from a man to make good my loss, or talk about him the way he talks about me, that makes me just the same kind of critter he is. Would you want me to be like that?"

I'd look at him, standing there so quietly, looking down at me with a thoughtful and faintly stern expression in his deep-set blue eyes, and I'd know that he was right. Papa was always right in his arguments. I didn't want him to be a thief and a liar and a gossipmonger. I really loved him best the way he was. And there was a certain satisfaction in knowing that, if he wanted to, he could lick the tar out of anyone else on the island. Still, I knew he was strong in more than just bone and muscle. He had a deeper strength that would never leave him. He was strong because he was not afraid. When he might bring in only a few dollars from his day's fishing or hauling, he didn't turn bitter. Daily he faced the long, slow battle to raise his family, to feed and clothe them adequately, and there was never an end to his patience, his humor, his interest in the world around him, and his tenderness toward his children.

Grandma
Anderson ~

Grandma was entirely the opposite of Grandpa in all ways. Where he was very dark, she was very fair, and where he was thin and bony, she was plump. She was extremely short, and almost seemed like the dumplings she used to stir up and drop into her kettles of soup. She must have been a sweet, doll-like creature in her youth, with her small, rosy mouth, her short nose, her bright blue eyes, her clusters of yellow curls. But when I knew her, she was simply Grandma, with the yellow hair—which never showed gray—strained back into a neat bun, a face as crinkled as an old russet apple, and many rustling petticoats. She was forever trotting busily around her kitchen, and would stand over her enormous breadboard and sing hymns in her strong accent as she looked out the window over the sink and watched the spray fly up from the dark, sea-drenched rocks of Eastern Harbor Point.

She was as strong in her religious beliefs as Grandpa, but I never heard her trying to pass them on to anyone else. She accomplished much more, as far as I was concerned, with her sweet singing, and the utter sincerity in her voice, as she crooned dreamily over her pots and pans and oven. When I heard her singing, "Vot a frand we haf in Yesus, all our sins and griefs to bear," I knew she believed it with all her heart and that the knowledge helped her to endure all the trials and hardships she had experienced.

She had come to this country when she was sixteen, little Anna Elmina Erickson of the bright blue eyes and yellow curls—like the crayon portrait in the sitting room. She had come to visit her married sister in Gloucester, and fully intended to go back to the little town near Stockholm where she was born and raised. But the ocean voyage had frightened her so that she never dared attempt to cross the Atlantic again. What longing she must have known for that country town and all her family that she was never to see again!

She was always busy with her knitting needles whenever she sat down for a moment to wait until the bread was baked, or in the intervals when the family was washing up for supper. She knit all her own stockings, and Grandpa's, and she must have knit hundreds of pairs of mittens. When I was twelve she taught me to knit a pair for myself. It was a hair-raising experience for us both.

In the open chamber of the big wood house [where wood for lobster traps was dried], I used to stand and look at her spinning wheel and wish I had seen her working it. But by the time I was old enough to climb the stairs of the wood house, there was no more need of carding and spinning wool, since mill-spun yarn was readily available.

She always seemed to be the meekest of women, and was quick to throw her apron over her head and cry whenever I had arguments with Grandpa, which occasions were frequent after I had grown past the stage when I didn't dare to answer back. It was a great age for me and a rough one for Grandpa when I decided to be heard as well as seen. It was hard to believe, when Grandma burst into tears because Grandpa and I were trying to stare each other down like a couple of Kilkenny cats, that there had once been a day when she defied Grandpa to the point of knocking him out with an iron mixing spoon.

When the children were small—my uncles, my mother, and Aunt Ellen—Grandpa would frighten his children into sitting down and being quiet by taking out his big clasp knife to sharpen it.

Whether he had ever told them he would cut their ears off, I don't know, but they were terrified of the knife, and they would sit in agonized stiffness, watching him pass the big shining blade back and forth over the whetstone.

It amazes me even now to think that Grandma, bending over a big pail of calf meal, stirring in hot water and skim milk with a huge mixing spoon, should have glanced up and caught the frightened eyes of her brood and known such instant fury that she straightened up quickly and struck out.

The spoon caught him on the forehead, just at the edge of his hair, and Grandpa went down like a falling spruce tree. According to the story—told by the children time and again long after they had grown up—she calmly picked up the knife, took it outdoors, and threw it as hard as she could into the alder swamp, where it was never found. Then she set to work to bring him around and stanch the blood from the wound.

Grandpa, of course, got himself another knife—a knife is a necessary tool—but he never again stood honing it while the children's frightened eyes watched in fascination. Strangest of all, he never upbraided Grandma for what she did with her big iron mixing spoon.

Grandma was taken with a shock in the summer of 1926. The stroke paralyzed her right side, but she recovered to the point where she could get out of bed and make her way around her home, fuss over her plants, and hold the calico cat in her lap. She was never able to perform any of her household tasks again, though, and Grandpa stopped lobstering and stayed home to be the housekeeper, wait on Grandma, and do the barn chores. My youngest uncle, Charlie, the only one of the children who lived at home now, earned the money to keep the home going.

Although in the past I'd greatly resented it when Grandpa leafed through the big Bible and made me listen to his reading, it always touched me deeply to see him sitting by the side of Grandma's bed, reading to her—in Swedish—and then getting down on his knees to pray. It would stir the heart of anyone to see those two old people, nodding together over the Scriptures, looking into each other's eyes, and suddenly breaking into tears. Though I couldn't understand the words they spoke, I knew by the way Grandma reached out with her good hand and touched Grandpa's that she was consoling him and he was consoling her.

When she was first stricken with the shock, she could not speak a single word, except the one syllable *me*. She would say that word, *me,* over and over, and break the hearts of all of us within hearing, as her eyes moved from one face to another and saw the bewilderment in each one.

While she was still unable to say more than that, it became evident that she was extremely worried about something. She would point to the west window of the sitting room, where she had her bed, frown very deeply, and say urgently, "Me, me, *me!*" And then she'd shake her head vehemently and say over again, "Me, me, me," but in a different tone. For days she did this, and when finally Aunt Ellen guessed what it was, Grandma's delighted face and eyes stabbed us with pain. "She doesn't want us to bury her on the mainland," said Aunt Ellen, and Grandma nodded happily in assent.

She died in 1930, and Grandpa waited ten years before he passed away, very quietly, in his sleep one sunny May afternoon. He had been a long time ailing, with headaches and a feebleness that held him back from the work that had been like life itself to him. "Work is the poor man's blessing," he used to tell us. When he couldn't do anything more, he died.

I looked on his face when he lay in the sitting room before the undertaker came, and I was profoundly amazed at the expression of deep peace on his face. A gentleness that was entirely foreign softened the features that had always been so harsh. And somehow I knew that the experience that Grandpa had dreaded all his life had not frightened him after all.

I thought of how he and Grandma had murmured to each other in the same room over their Bible, and how he had knelt and prayed aloud when all she could say in response was, "Me, me," and make it so expressive of all she felt.

Their favorite psalm seems to have been the Twenty-third, and since then, when I pick up the worn old Bible that was once theirs and turn over the pages printed in both English and Swedish, I can almost hear Grandpa's voice, trembling with emotion that brought tears to his eyes.

"The Lord is my shepherd. I shall not want."

And then Grandma's softly murmured, "Me, me."

The syllables are not the same, but I knew she was really saying—as I'd so often heard her say—"*Ja, ja.*"

Self-Defense ～

When we had fights with the neighborhood children, Mama never had to be coaxed to join in the fray, but Papa was always uncooperative whenever we arrived home beaten and asking for help.

"It's your fight," he'd say. "You'll have to handle it."

Even if we were outnumbered, he'd still insist that it was for us to figure out the ways and means of winning the battle.

At one time my principal enemy was a boy who was older than I, but smaller, since he was slim and wiry and I was on the stocky side. He infuriated me by standing off where I could not reach him, making all manner of remarks to inform everyone within hearing that I was uncouth, dishonest, and immoral. Being a boy of no wit and small intelligence, he made remarks that were short and to the point.

Warren was courageous enough to make some of his statements where my mother could hear him, and although she paid little attention to his opinions on my honesty and tidiness, she was vastly concerned with my moral standing. Because he came out boldly with his assurances that I had been out in the woods with him for no good purpose, she thought there must be some truth in it. No matter how much I denied it, with tears and many furious threats to get even with him, she continued to eye me with suspicion. Mama was seldom convinced that the fear of punishment, or any more fastidious reasons, could be a deterrent where natural instincts were concerned.

She was noncommittal when I swore I hated Warren. She just narrowed her eyes, and after I had gone over all the things I detested about him, all but choking in my disgust, she would say flatly, "Well, if he's such a terrible boy, what do you have him hanging around your playhouse for?"

She remained unconvinced when I said he never set foot inside the playhouse, but we couldn't stop him from standing off a little way, watching us and tossing out uncomplimentary remarks, which I tried to ignore. We couldn't drive him out of the woods—they didn't belong to us.

The weak link in my evidence was that it was my self-imposed task to go away from the playhouse to gather fern roots, spruce tips, berries, or whatever I could find for play food. And sometimes I took walks by myself to the shores to search for boards and boxes to add to our shelves and cupboards. On these occasions, no one could swear that I'd been alone, that Warren hadn't been with me, and Mama could not believe that Warren would dare to come out openly with such insinuations if they weren't true.

I could believe anything of Warren. He knew that whatever he said made trouble for me, and since he wasn't strong enough to win a fistfight or a wrestling match with me, he took his own way to get revenge. His father whipped him frequently, and I knew he must be rugged, in spite of his slenderness, to endure all the punishment he took at home. The occasions when I could catch him and beat him up had little effect on him except to make him hate me more.

In the fall the playhouse feud stopped, but our battles simply moved to different turf. He had to go for milk to the Rhodes farm, and so did I, so the journey across the island was enlivened by flying rocks, loud insults, and much weeping on Warren's part if I could catch him and scratch him with my fingernails, which I purposely kept at a good, useful length.

Finally he enlisted my cousin Helen to fight on his side. Helen and I had our moments when we disliked each other actively and passionately, but after a quarrel we would make up again and invite each other back and forth between the playhouses. These ceremonial visits usually turned out to be occasions for looking over things critically, with the intention to come back later when the playhouse was unguarded and steal whatever was the most desirable.

Warren approached Helen during one of our intervals of hatred. I didn't know it until a night in October when I was walking along in the quiet, frost-scented dusk, swinging my tin milk pail and whistling to keep the spooks away. I noted, trying to be casual about it, that the long fish house above the beach seemed to loom very high against the sky as I went by it, and the open doorways were very black and mysterious. Trying not to think of what they might possibly contain besides bait butts, I paid little attention to the high bows of the boats hauled up close on the other side of the path, so I was taken completely unaware when two small figures leaped out from behind a boat and fell upon me. Each had a good stout lath, and they beat me with vigor. I had nothing but the little tin pail, and I swung out with it, but it did no good. I was unable to get by their swinging laths, so I turned and ran home, to the accompaniment of wild laughter on their part.

I was so mad that I didn't feel my scrapes and bruises. I blamed Warren most of all. I was sure that he had worked out the plan to ambush me. He knew he couldn't have done much by himself—I would have waded in past his blows—but he'd guessed that I'd be fairly helpless against two laths whacking at me in the dark. I could just imagine how superior he felt and how he and Helen must be sneering at me. This choked me with rage. I stamped into the house and loudly asserted that I wasn't going after any more milk if I couldn't walk along the road without being held up by a couple of yellow cowards who had to jump out at me with sticks.

Mama and Papa were both upset, and Mama was going to go with me when I set out again, but Papa wouldn't let her.

"You can't go everywhere with her all her life, Agnes," he said. "She's got to fight her own battles."

"But I can't fight the two of them at once," I wailed. "'Specially when they have clubs!"

"I thought they had laths," he said solemnly, looking at me over the bowl of his corncob pipe.

"Well, you might as well call a lath a club," I grumbled, "if you get it on the top of your head in the dark when you're not looking."

He smiled, a twinkling kind of smile that was mostly in his eyes, and puffed away at his pipe. I had set the pail down on the table and was peeling off my coat.

"You're going for that milk," he said quietly. "No use to take your coat off."

"But they'll lay for me again," I protested.

"Well, wait a little while, and they'll have gone home and won't bother you."

"Is that the way I'll have to do it every night?" I cried. "They'll be holding me up in broad daylight next!"

"Tomorrow night you can settle your score with them," he promised.

So I waited around the kitchen for a little while, then went for my milk. I walked quietly and watched all shadows, and crept up on any likely place where they might be hiding, but nothing happened, and I got back home again unmolested.

The next day I had to take a lot of sly laughs from both of them, but I had sense enough to say nothing, and they refrained from making any remarks about the night before. I imagine they were both surprised that neither of my parents spoke of the matter to their parents.

That evening Papa took me out to the woodpile before I set off with my milk pail, and said, "Now, if they want to fight with sticks, and it's two against one, the only thing you can do is get the surprise on them—with a bigger stick." He handed me a split barrel stave, a piece of wood about five feet long and small enough around for my hand to grasp firmly.

"I don't go for fighting," he said sternly, "but there are times when you just have to do it, or else you have no peace. Now you go along and get it over with. Don't be afraid to hit hard, and don't be fussy about where you hit."

Mama didn't know what he was telling me, or that he'd given me the split barrel stave for a weapon. She was still arguing that either she or Papa should go along the road with me and give Helen and Warren a good talking-to, but Papa only shook his head and sent me off. "Go along now and don't be afraid. Remember, their heads are just as tender as yours."

I didn't whistle as I walked along; I tried to be as stealthy as an Indian, and when I came to the line of boats hauled up at the edge of the path in front of the long fish house, I slowed down and listened hard. Finally, above the soft swash of water on the shore, I heard a subdued giggle and a murmured word or two, and knew they were waiting for me to come down the path, with my feet betraying me as I kicked a pebble or stepped on a stick in the darkness.

I tiptoed closer, and then I stood on the other side of the high bow behind which they were hiding, and I could hear them gloating over the way they would surprise me again.

I leaped around the bow, arriving in their midst like a typhoon, flaying on all sides with my split barrel stave. As Papa had told me to do, I laid it on with a will, and in the excitement and exhilaration of knowing this was one fight that was legitimate, I did not even feel their return blows, which had no more effect on me than if they'd beaten me with feathers. I struck swift and hard, and my weapon must have hurt them far more than theirs had hurt me the night before. The surprise element also had a devastating effect on them. They ran down the beach yelling in panic, and I stood alone, triumphant, listening to Warren shrieking, "You wait till I tell my father on you!"

I strode along jauntily, swinging my milk pail, feeling very happy. I had put them on the run, the way they'd done to me, but I had come out further ahead because I had fought them alone.

When I returned home with the milk I heard men's voices in the kitchen, and one of them was raised angrily. It belonged to Warren's father. For a moment I was afraid, but only for a moment. Papa was there too.

When Warren's father saw me he turned with his eyes flashing. "You beat up my kid tonight, didn't ye? Don't lie, now!"

"She doesn't have to lie about it," said Papa calmly. "I told her to do it."

Warren's father was too astonished to explode at once. "You *told* her to?"

"I certainly did. I can't go around protecting her from your boy, Ralph. And when he gets someone to lie in wait and then jump out on her when she comes along, I think she should do something to protect herself, don't you?"

His voice was very mild but his eyes weren't. Mama was standing by the stove with her hand on the lifter, trying to get a word in. But Ralph wasn't listening to her; he was just looking at Papa, struggling to find words.

"Then you admit she pounded my boy up tonight, Herman?" he asked, and his face was very red.

"That's right," said Papa. "And I hope she gave him plenty, so he'll know enough not to bother her again."

"By God, I'll teach her!" Ralph said. "She needs a damn good lickin', and if you don't give it to her, I will!"

"Oh, no, Ralph," said Papa. His voice wasn't so mild now.

"By God, I will! She beat my kid with a club! And you're goin' to let her git away with it!"

"How about your boy beating up my girl with a stick, and having someone else help him?" inquired Papa, setting his pipe on the stove shelf and looking hard at Ralph. "Is that fair?"

"They didn't have sticks," said Ralph, "and they didn't hurt her any. If they did, she could've come to me and told me about it, but she didn't, so I guess she ain't so bad off. But she's a devil, that one." He glared at me. "She needs a wallopin', but I can't expect you to give it to her. You never do."

Ralph shouldn't have said that. Papa didn't like to hear reflections on the way he brought up his family. It was true, he didn't like to punish us; the neighbors knew it as well as we did. He wasn't like Mama, who lost her temper with us often. She was the one we could wheedle, however—the one who most frequently gave in to us.

Papa was the one who believed everything we told him. He insisted on honesty, and we knew the consequences if we lied to him. So we told the truth and were believed. He didn't like the neighbors to imply that he was aiding and abetting his children in the practice of mischief and bad manners.

"I believe what Dorothy told me," Papa stated.

"I believe what Warren told me," said Ralph. They faced each other like a couple of roosters all ready to jump each other.

"And I told her she had to defend herself in the only way she could," said Papa. "And if that means she has to carry a club with her, then that's what she'll have to do." He clamped his jaws together tightly, and looked austere and forbidding.

"She ain't beatin' up my kid and gettin' away with it!" Ralph warned him.

"Then he'll have to mind his business and let her walk unmolested," said Papa in his finest language.

"You and your damn talk," said Ralph.

"I can do something else besides talk," said Papa, and began to roll up his sleeves. "Just step out here into the yard a minute, and maybe we can settle this once and for all."

Mama began trotting her foot and said, "Herman—"

Ralph watched Papa warily. He wasn't so tall as Papa, but he was as big in every other way, and as strong. Mama was scared, but I was excited. I was going to enjoy seeing Ralph get a licking. It was almost as good as giving Warren what he deserved.

Ralph said, after a moment, "I guess there ain't no need for us to fight over it, Herman." He smiled appeasingly.

"There isn't," Papa agreed. "And I don't blame you for believing Warren. Naturally he's going to do the best he can to get your sympathy. But I'll tell you, Ralph, I have to send my girl on errands, and if she can't go on her way without running into your boy and having trouble, then they'll have to fight it out. And if he wins, she'll have to take her medicine, same as he did tonight. Let them alone. They'll straighten it out between them. You'll see."

Ralph looked at him and then at me, and the glance he gave me wasn't good. He knew as well as I did that Warren couldn't lick me all by himself. I have no doubt that if Warren had stood up doggedly to me in a fight, he would have had more success, but he always ran and cried, and then took his revenge by calling dirty names from a distance.

"Well, there ain't no harm in her comin' to me if Warren bothers her, is there?" Ralph asked Papa.

"None at all," said Papa in a courtly manner.

Ralph scowled at me. "Will you come to me if you kids get into trouble again?"

I nodded.

"All right, then." He looked around at Papa and Mama. "Hope there ain't no hard feelin's over this. I know how kids are to stir up things."

"Everything's all right, Ralph," said Papa. "I'm glad you came and talked to me." I was glad too. It had done my heart good to see Papa start rolling up his sleeves.

Ralph went home, and Papa looked at me with a quizzical expression in his blue eyes. "Did you hit hard?" he asked.

"I hit good and hard," I said.

"Now that's a fine thing," said Mama in disgust. "So *that's* what you were telling her out by the woodpile! Telling her to go out and fight like a—a—I don't know what! That's no way to bring up a girl, Herman, and you know it!"

"What's she going to do?" he asked mildly. "Be scared of her own shadow and hide when she sees trouble? Oh, no. Not if I have anything to do with it."

He turned to me sternly. "Mind you, I don't want to hear of you *starting* anything. Don't get *that* idea in your head. But if somebody else starts something and you have to fight, I don't want to hear of you running away like a coward. You understand?"

I nodded. He didn't have to worry. I could look out for myself now.

Temptations at
the Store ~

The village store, which had been in existence even before Papa had come to the island with his two brothers, still carried on an extensive business while I was growing up. The Cries had started the store, and a Crie was still carrying on. He was "Uncle" Eben to all of us, and a more genial uncle could never be found. He always had a smile and a little jingle for us children, and the one he seemed to like best went like this:

> *If you save up your money,*
> *And pile up your rocks,*
> *Then you'll always have tobacco*
> *In your old tobacco box.*

His little rhyme never taught us to save our pennies, of course. The array of peppermint sticks, chocolate drops, gumdrops, and round, hard candies like bright marbles made us deaf to his promises of all the things one might own if one's tobacco box were full.

Uncle Eben was no great businessman; he had no thought of getting rich from his store. It was something to do, something that had always been going on. He was merely taking his turn at standing behind the counter, measuring molasses from the barrel in the back room, weighing out sugar or crackers, slicing off hunks of cheese from the great wheel that always stood on the jackknife-scarred counter. He never seemed to be out of patience with us, no matter how long we stood with our noses against the glass of the showcase. He knew just how much careful planning it took to get the most out of a penny; the candy must go far and leave a lingering taste in our mouths. He would stand there waiting, humming behind his drooping mustache.

He always wore a brown derby, and that alone would have set him apart from the fishermen who traded at his store. Only a few of them wore derbies, black ones, and only when they were dressed up. Uncle Eben wore his all the time, indoors and out. It was a part of him, like his kindliness, his smile, his patience with us when we couldn't make up our minds about how our pennies were to be spent.

Uncle Eben ran the post office too. The mailboat landed at a big wharf near the store, and boat-day was a busy and exciting time. Everybody came to watch the freight being taken off and wheeled into the store. The mailbags were always slung with a flourish into a little room at the back, and dark green curtains were drawn across the big, wide window so nobody could watch Uncle Eben sort out the mail. An array of pigeonholes received the mail, and through a gap in the curtains we'd sometimes catch a glimpse of Uncle Eben's hand as it poked a letter into its proper place. It was exciting to peer into the pigeonhole that held your own mail and wonder who'd sent the card or letter it held. And above the rustle and thump of the packages and letters, above the murmur of those who stood around in the store waiting for the sorting to be finished, you could always hear an occasional fragment of the jingle Uncle Eben was humming.

Only a few men on the island drank in those days, but they all smoked—except Uncle Eben. He was a bachelor. He had none of the cares and anxieties that beset a family man. When he went home at night, he could sit down and relax. He could read his paper and look down at the harbor or across Camp Cove to Matinicus Rock Light and be very peaceful up there in the Crie Homestead. He made enough money to keep him comfortable. The kindly, quizzical smile was always in his eyes and around his mouth, except perhaps when the older boys stole corn from his garden for a corn-roast or took his old horse, Bess, out for a bareback ride at night when she was supposed to be resting in the paddock behind the big red barn. But Uncle Eben's smile would soon come back. He had been a boy once himself.

Uncle Eben didn't like to have business rush too fast. It upset him to find a certain brand of goods selling too quickly. That meant he would have to send another order before he'd expected to. So when he got a brand that was superior and was sold out within a week, he wouldn't order that kind again. Instead, he'd get something that was not so popular. If you asked him why he didn't have more of the special kind, he'd shake his head and say, "Goes too fast! Didn't hardly have time to put it up on the shelves!"

As his was the only store on the island for many years, he did not have to worry about competition, and if you didn't like what he had on the shelves, you didn't have to buy. It wouldn't hurt you to get along without it anyway, he said. People had too many fancy things nowadays that "Wahn't good for 'em." People were happier when they didn't have to buy so much to make them content. That was the way he lived and the way he believed, and he seemed happy enough.

Naturally, because he was a merchant, Uncle Eben got all kinds of advertisements, and one day I saw what seemed to be a postcard lying on the counter beside the big round of cheese. It had a beautiful picture on it: a girl in a white middy blouse, holding two crossed signal flags. She was pink-cheeked and beautiful, with blonde curly hair, and just my opposite. I had no illusions; I was short and plump, and dark as a gypsy with my tanned skin and straight dark hair. I suppose I must have looked at the postcard girl with envy. She wore a beautiful snowy white middy blouse. I had middy blouses, but they didn't seem to have the chaste elegance of this one, and I never could keep mine from getting smudged as soon as I'd put them on.

I studied the card covetously and then turned it over. It was an advertisement for chocolates. Then Uncle Eben came out from the back room with the molasses I'd ordered, and I asked him if the card was any good.

He took it, examined it carefully, read the words on the back, and said, "No, guess 'tain't. Jest an ad for candy. Ain't goin' to git none of it, though. Too expensive."

Why I didn't ask him for the card then and there I don't know, except that I remember thinking I was too big a girl to be asking for an old postcard advertisement. So I went out with the molasses and walked home. But I wanted that card. I thought it was just the thing to tack up in my room, along with a rotogravure of the Prince of Wales. I wanted that card so badly, and yet was so ashamed to ask Uncle Eben for it that when I had to go back to the store on another errand and saw the card still lying on the counter, I slipped it into my pocket when Uncle Eben wasn't looking.

When I got home I proudly showed it to Mama and the children, and to Papa, who was sitting in his Morris chair reading a magazine. Mama just glanced at it; the other children were suitably impressed, but Papa said, "Where'd you get it?"

My guilty conscience betrayed me. I hesitated when I said it was just an old card Uncle Eben had said was no good. "He didn't want it for anything," I added.

"Did you ask him for it?" said Papa. "Did he give it to you?"

"Well, not exactly," I hedged, my feet beginning to fidget. Papa's eyes had that effect on me. "I just asked him if it was any good, and he said no. I didn't really ask him for it." By then I was sure that Papa must be thinking what I was afraid Uncle Eben would have thought— that I was too big a girl to want an old postcard. I was embarrassed, but Papa thought I was blushing for another reason.

"If you didn't ask for it," he said slowly, "and he didn't give it to you, then you've just the same as stolen it." The words fell on my ears like the tolling of funeral bells. Papa was accusing me of *theft*. But the next words were worse, if possible. "You'll have to take it back."

"Oh, I couldn't!" I burst out, aghast. Supposing someone was in the store when I went back with it! I'd just die if I had to talk about that card with somebody listening. It would be bad enough to have to explain to Uncle Eben alone, even if he didn't get mad about it.

"You'll take that card back," said Papa, "if I have to lead you by the ear all the way to the store."

I knew he meant it. Papa could be lenient with me when I took his hatchet and nicked the sharp blade a dozen times. He would let me off with a mild scolding when I took his best hammer and lost it, or used up all his trap nails. But when it came to something like this, he was stern and cold and unyielding.

Mama said placatingly, "Don't be so hard on her, Herman. You take the card back when you go to the store."

"I didn't take it," he said. "Why should I take it back? That's for her to do. She knows it's not right to take things without asking."

I looked down at the card. It was an insignificant scrap of paper now, not worth all the shame and embarrassment that was parboiling me at the moment.

"Go on." Papa commanded. "Don't just stand there. Take that card back."

"I'll take it tomorrow," I said. Early in the morning, I thought, when nobody would be likely to come in.

"*Now!*" he said. We all jumped. I made one last despairing effort.

"But it's just an old card—Uncle Eben won't know it's gone!"

"*You* know it's gone," he said. "And that's enough. Now I'm not going to argue about this. Hurry up. Beat it!" He half-rose from his chair as though he would go with me, and I knew well enough that if he did go, he'd have me by the ear as he'd promised. That would be the biggest humiliation of all, because I was a big girl of twelve, and no little pindling mite with her wits not quite all about her.

I started back to the store without another word. The path was miles long, it seemed, and I couldn't hope that Uncle Eben had gone home. Papa would send me home after him, and Uncle Eben's brother

John and his wife, Nancy, with whom Eben lived, would be standing around to listen to me confess that I'd stolen something, and not even anything worthwhile.

There were customers in the store, so I lingered in the background, hot and miserable, until they'd gone. Then he came to the counter and leaned over it encouragingly.

I drew the card out of my pocket and laid it on the counter.

"I took this without asking for it," I said stiffly. "Papa made me bring it back."

He took the card and turned it over. "And wouldn't you have returned it by yourself?" he asked gently.

I was too ashamed to answer. I could only stare at him, while my face burned. Then he smiled a little. "I'm sure you would have brought it back by yourself. I never knew you to take anything before. But you brought it back, so it's all right."

I still didn't say anything. I was too sorry. I had debased myself, and it was horrible. "I still wish you'd asked me for it," he said. "I'd've been glad to give it to you, but what ain't worth asking for ain't worth having." He tore the card in two and dropped it to the floor at his feet.

"Don't be ashamed to ask for anything you want," he told me, leaning his arms on the glass candy counter. "It's not begging to ask for anything. It's just being kind of—well, polite. I guess that's what you'd call it. It shows you have regard for what belongs to somebody else."

"I won't ever do anything like that again," I said humbly, and turned to go out.

"I'm sure you won't," he said. I shut the door behind me very softly, and walked home almost as slowly as I'd come. I was thinking that neither Papa nor Uncle Eben would have to worry about my ever again taking anything without asking. My first attempt had filled me with a sense of shame I would never forget. The little card hadn't been worth the price I'd had to pay. I realized then that nothing gained in such a fashion is worth the bill that comes later.

LEFT: Dot with her mother, about age two.

BELOW: The Criehaven Campfire Girls. Dot is in the center.

Dot + Mama
Mama's Darling

Criehaven harbor in the early 1900s, showing the Crie wharf and the long shop building that housed fishermen upstairs and their supplies downstairs.

ABOVE: Young Neil Simpson learning the lobstering trade from his uncle and grandfather.

LEFT: Dot's family rented rooms in this house from 1913 to 1918.

ABOVE: The Simpson family in 1917. Dot (age 12) is standing in back. In front are Ruth (7), Herman, Oram (5), and Agnes holding Evelyn (2).

RIGHT: One of Dot's few formal photographs, perhaps taken while she was on the mainland going to high school.

FACING PAGE, BOTTOM: Dories similar to the one Dot loved to row. Her father's dory was about fifteen feet long

The head of the harbor in the early 1900s. Dot's brother Oscar later owned the house in the center, and her father lived for a while in the small camp on the far right before buying a small house farther down the shore.

ABOVE: Anna and Carl Anderson, Dot's maternal grandparents, in the 1920s.

RIGHT: Criehaven's fishermen in the early 1920s. Herman Simpson is standing second from right. His brother Alfred is farthest right. Guy Simpson, Dot's future husband, is on the left end of the front row, seated on the ground. On the right end of the same row, looking shy, is Dot's brother Oram.

ABOVE: Guy and Dot in 1927 or 1928. They were married in December 1927.

LEFT: Carl Anderson in 1904. In 1900 he'd been invited to move his family from Matinicus to Crie-haven so the school would have enough pupils to stay open.

Dot's family in later years.

ABOVE, LEFT TO RIGHT: Agnes in 1955, in Rockland. She died later that year. Evelyn in 1942, visiting from Connecticut. Madelyn (Mary) in 1940, married and living on Matinicus. Bette (Gertrude) sometime in the 1940s. (No photo available for Ruth.)

RIGHT: Dot's brothers in 1948, Criehaven fishermen all. Left to right: Neil, Oscar, Oram, and Russell.

ABOVE: Dot loved to whittle, making thousands of miniature lobster buoys, among other items. Note the netting "needles" (shuttles) behind her head.

BELOW: Successful authors Elisabeth Ogilvie (left) and Dot Simpson posed with their latest potboilers in 1956.

Stepfather ~

I was twelve when I learned that Papa wasn't my real father—that my own father lived somewhere else and had never seen me. It was a heartbreaking discovery, and it came out of mockery, the cruel teasing that so often goes on in the schoolyard. One of the girls, who was almost my own age, began to taunt me, saying, "You're not Dorothy Simpson! Herman Simpson isn't your father! You don't know who your father is!"

We'd all been shouting back and forth, and I considered this simply a new way to get under my skin. It worked; I was infuriated.

"Do you know who it is, if you're so smart?" I asked, thinking that of course it was just teasing, and she'd simply keep on repeating what she'd already said until she was tired of it. Instead, she nodded her pigtails and looked wise.

"Who is it?" I demanded.

"Go home and ask your mother."

"You're a liar," I told her. "I don't believe you."

She only smiled smugly. "Go ask your mother—*she* ought to know who he is!"

Somehow I couldn't shrug this off. I did ask Mama when I went home at noontime. I asked her simply to be reassured. To my amazement, she sat down in the rocking chair and began to cry. I was immediately angry—on two counts: Here was something mysterious that I couldn't possibly understand, and here was Mama crying instead of calling my schoolmate a liar. If she'd been stern and cold-eyed and had said, "Somebody is telling you lies," I would have dismissed the whole thing from my mind. But there she sat, crying silently and staring out of the window, and not giving me a bit of explanation.

After a while I said nervously, "Isn't Papa...Papa?"

She didn't look at me, just shook her head. "No."

"Then who *is* it?" My voice broke away from me, and I almost shouted. A strange panic, an entirely new feeling, had seized me, and I wanted to kick and strike, to hurt something or somebody. There was a tight, burning ache in my throat, and I was somehow frightened.

"He never saw you," she said. "He went away before you were born and never came back." I felt rage hardening in me the same way my fists were hardening. I wanted to go out and choke somebody. I didn't care especially who it was, but it would have been good to get hold of the one who could make Mama look as she looked now. It was such a sad expression, so deeply unhappy, that I thought I couldn't bear it. "Your name isn't Simpson," she said. "It's Knowlton."

I opened my mouth to say something, but she shook her head. "Don't ask me anything more," she said. "It happened a long time ago. It's best to forget it."

"But how can I forget it?" I said. "Nobody else is forgetting it. If they did, nobody would tease me about it now."

"I know," she said gently. "But don't mind what anybody says. It's no crime for you to have a stepfather. And if anybody says anything to you again, just laugh at them. They can't hurt you, not really. If they say your name's not Simpson, just say, 'I know it.' They'll get tired of teasing you if you don't let them think it bothers you."

I looked at her without speaking. That was all very easy to say, but not so easy to believe. It wasn't a crime to have a stepfather, but I didn't want a stepfather—I'd always believed Herman Simpson was my real father. It was a shock to find that he wasn't. It put me off balance; I couldn't look at things right, and nothing seemed to be where it belonged. I felt like an alien in the familiar kitchen.

Ruth and Oram and Evelyn and Russell belonged to Papa and Mama. I belonged to just Mama. I only half-belonged to my family. Part of me was somewhere else, and that part of me was like something dead; it had no reason, no aim, no foundation. It was something adrift, cast loose with nothing to guide it. All the things I had thought about myself in relation to Papa were of no consequence. While I thought he was good and intelligent, I could not hope to be the same. I could inherit nothing from him; his blood wasn't in me. The other children could receive not only the color of their eyes and hair and the shape of their noses from him, but his ways and mannerisms as well. Never could I expect such things. They were his, but I could have no part of them. I could only inherit from Mama and the unknown who lived somewhere in the distances beyond Criehaven.

I had to return to school and assume a nonchalance I didn't feel and acknowledge a name that had no meaning. Outwardly I was the same, but from that moment I felt a barrier between me and the others. They could all belong wholly to a family, but I couldn't. When they wrote their names on their lesson papers, they were writing what was true, but I wasn't.

I was still to use the name Simpson, because it had become a habit with everyone and with me, and after that one instance in the schoolyard, the matter of names never came out into the open again. The younger children were not conscious of the barrier; it belonged to me alone. I could not get away from the haunting knowledge. It filled me with sadness, and for a long time I lived with such loneliness that it seemed to have become a permanent part of me.

I didn't belong to Papa.

The knowledge colored my thinking for a long time, until I could adjust myself and realize that, no matter who my own father might be, I was fortunate in having Herman Simpson for a stepfather. That was much better than not having him for any sort of parent at all.

Papa talked to me about my own father and told me not to feel upset about it. He pointed out to me that, as far as he was concerned, I was really his own. Maybe the way he taught me and told me things, and was so lenient and patient with me, was his way of trying to prove to me that he meant it.

He was a strong family man, and his children came first always. He knew well enough that he would never be able to supply them with much of the world's goods, but he tried to give them understanding, to teach them a way of life and conduct that he felt would enable them to be self-respecting citizens when they came of age.

He was a man who used much profanity, but he was not really profane. He could swear long and loudly when he was angry, but when he sat down to talk to me he was in the habit of using such phrases as "Vengeance is mine, saith the Lord," "The Lord will provide," and "Do unto others as you would have them do unto you."

"Live by the Ten Commandments and the Golden Rule," he advised us frequently, "and you'll have nothing to fear, either from your conscience or from any other human being."

Papa was rigidly honest, no matter who persecuted him. I figured that a person who stole would never understand what it meant when his victim turned the other cheek; the only lesson for a thief was the theft of something *he* treasured. I flew into a rage whenever Papa refused to retaliate. He would say, simply, "Nothing a man steals will ever do him any good." Then he would go his serene way as if it did not mean a thing to have his only axe disappear, or a bunch of his tarred trap heads go from his workshop bench, or his traps come up empty because someone else had already hauled them.

He knew well enough who stole from him; in a tiny community like ours it was impossible not to know every movement, every act, and to guess correctly what each meant. But when I argued violently with Papa, he would only look off toward the horizon, puffing at his pipe, and then say very gently, "Two wrongs never make a right." His stock of platitudes used to infuriate me, especially when I was in a temper anyway. But before I could burst out again, he'd go on. "If a man steals from me, that's one wrong committed— if I steal from him, that's another wrong. But that doesn't take care of the matter." He would puff away some more and then add, "If I can't come by things honestly, then I don't want anything. I'd rather starve than steal."

"But what about us kids?" I'd cry out. I'd feel so exasperated, I'd resent his tranquillity. I couldn't ever understand why he could go around with empty pockets and see others prospering with what they'd taken from him. I was choked with fury when I saw someone openly using our axe. I'd want to claim it, but Papa would say, "No, don't fight over it. If that man is so poor he can't buy an axe, and he has to lower himself to the place where he'd steal from me, then he's twice as poor."

That didn't make sense to me. It all sounded very fine, but I just wanted the axe back.

Over and over Papa tried to impress us with the necessity of having pride. And if that meant we couldn't take back what belonged to us or reply in kind to adults who made slurring remarks, we didn't think we wanted any. But we had to have pride, whether we wanted it or not, for whenever he found out that we'd broken his rules, it meant instant punishment. He might let us slide by with a reprimand when we ran off and played instead of doing our chores or used his hatchet and dulled the edge or broke off teeth from the saw, but it was more than a reprimand we got if he found out that we'd touched anything belonging to anyone else or were saucy to older people.

When he was trying to imbue me with the desire to become an upright and self-respecting member of the island community, he showered me abundantly with aphorisms. "Birds of a feather flock together," he would instruct me with a gravity that really made the words impressive. "You're known by the company you keep." Or, "Water seeks its own level." And his prime favorite: "When your good name is gone, you have nothing left." He might not have known what Shakespeare said on the subject, but he had the same thought and forced it irrevocably upon us.

Usually we didn't want to listen, but we were obliged to. And when I could really consider myself an adult, I found that he had been telling the truth, after all. Though I hadn't been very much impressed when he was trying to keep me from being a complete pagan, I had absorbed his ideas in spite of myself. Even now I can remember how he looked as he talked, how kindly he watched us to be sure we understood him. He must be relieved to know that we haven't forgotten.

He used to sit and talk to me in the evenings when Mama was away on the mainland for her next new baby, and although he knew he could do little to further them, he had great hopes for his boys and girls. He had no specific plans; he simply wanted them to do what was right, to be a credit to him and his teachings, to hold fast to each other, and to give each other the aid and understanding he would not be there to give them when they were men and women grown. He was fond of leaning back in his chair and staring up at the ceiling as he smoked and I washed the supper dishes. He would talk in his quiet, peaceful way, as if he were thinking aloud.

"I'm an ignorant man in a lot of ways—I've never had much education, and I've never been anywhere to speak of—but I want my kids to have schooling and get the things out of life that education can bring 'em. I want them to do and see the things I couldn't do and see... But most of all, I guess, I want them to be decent, law-abiding citizens. I don't want them ever to profit by harming others. And more'n all that, I want them to be kind to each other and give a helping hand when the going's rough."

I've never forgotten these things he wanted for us, but I've never remembered them more poignantly than when two of his sons were on Guadalcanal and another, as captain of his own Coast Guard patrol boat, was on duty around the very island and over the very bay that Papa had loved so much. And when they came back from the service to go into lobstering again, taking up where they left off when the war started, I thought of Papa and the heartbreakingly tiny sums of money he'd earned, for his sons were making between one and two hundred dollars a day. When I saw the boys in their big, new, shining boats crossing Penobscot Bay in speed and comfort when they wanted to go ashore, I thought of Papa, working in the cold and wet, the icy spray drenching his thin, tanned face, the wind and sea buffeting the little old boat that was too small and rotten-timbered for him to go very far from the island. When I see one of the boys casually taking a hundred-dollar bill from a bulging wallet, I think how flat his worn billfold always was and know that he had probably never touched a hundred-dollar bill in his life.

Papa was never bitter about his own situation, for he felt that he was rich in children, and he had faith in the future of those children. At the moment, it seems as if his faith had been justified. Yes, he was a family man, and his children were his true wealth. And next to his wife and family he loved Criehaven. Perhaps his love for it was something I inherited from him, after all. Every one of Herman Simpson's children feels that it is the most wonderful island on the Maine coast. It is Home, though many of us live away from it now and can only see it when we bring it into our mind's eye.

A tiny island, Criehaven stands rocky and forbidding on a windy day when the ocean lashes its shores, dreamlike and beautiful when the ocean is calm and the island seems to lie on the shining blue surface like an uncut jewel. It was Papa's home for more than forty years—a fitting nest for a gentle eagle and his brood.

Fine Days for Fishing ~

While Russell was still a baby [1918], we moved from the three rooms into a whole house in another section of the settlement, not far from the schoolhouse. It was very small, and the kitchen was hardly big enough for us to turn around in. This in itself was a big disadvantage. Also, the well was a good distance from the house, and getting the water was one of my chores. Despite the big rainwater barrel to help out with the washing, it seemed to me that the two pails that stood on the dresser by the kitchen sink were always empty. I was forever being sent around the curve of the beach and up to the village well. I got to the point where I glared threateningly at any child who asked innocently for a drink of water.

The harbor took on a whole new aspect from this new place. Although there was a little spruce-covered rise behind the house, there were no tall trees like the ones we'd left behind. We could look across the village and see them, saw-toothed and dark against the sky, and sigh for the playhouses they had sheltered. We no longer had all the long, rugged, rocky western shore nearby to roam over, and no flat fields around us good for a game of catch, or tag—just rocky ledge and beach rocks almost to the doorstep, and a swamp. On the other side of the little rise stood the schoolhouse.

But we also could see more intimately the doings of the fishermen as they worked around the wharf and in and out of their fish houses. We could see all the dories, skiffs, and peapods tied up on the beach. In the early mornings it was fun to hear the gulls calling as they walked around on the pebbles at the edge of the tide and to see the men pulling their baitboxes down the beach to their dories and skiffs before rowing out to their boats, leaving silver tracks across the water in the early sunlight. It was nice to listen to the sound of the sea so close to the house, to go to sleep to it and awaken to it. The crying of the gulls was more personal, for they practically lived around the wharf and the fish houses, always busy looking for old bait or the fresh herring that the seining crew brought home.

There was a drawback to being so close to the active part of the harbor: It wasn't so easy for me to run off and go fishing when I should have been ironing clothes or cleaning up my room. I couldn't take a rowboat and go off by myself when I should have been washing dishes. I could never get out from under Mama's eye now, and whatever I wanted to do, I had to do brazenly—no more sneaking off, no more evasive explanations. I could not hope to saunter off, looking down at the ground as if I were searching for something I'd lost, and then get out of sight behind a building and race for the shore. Now, when I started toward the beach, she would see me; and when she called to me, I would surely hear it; and if I kept on without looking back, then I was disobeying openly, no doubt about it.

In order to get away from the house more, it appeared necessary for me to cultivate Papa's company, which meant I insisted on going to help him in his work. It was infinitely delightful to be with him in the little workshop where he built his traps, or in the long bait house. He rented a small section in the bait house to keep his big hogsheads of salted herring. I adored the smell of good bait, and I never shied away from baiting-up, even though I always developed a multitude of itches when my hands were in the bait. I discovered that it was practically impossible to scratch behind the ear with only the tip of one finger without getting a smear of the lovely, ripe stuff in my hair. But I didn't refrain from scratching, and Mama always knew where I'd been before I got as much as one foot through the door.

On fine days, I begged to go hauling or fishing with Papa. When I went hauling, I was no help. It was really a joy ride, because all I did was lie on the forward deck and dream the hours away while he pulled his traps and baited them. But when we went fishing, I could help, because I loved to fish and I could catch my share.

Those days so far back in childhood were possessed of a rare and satisfying charm. Papa loved fishing too, and I think he got much more out of the peaceful hours than the price of the fish he took back to the wharf. He was perfectly content to sit for hours on the top of his little engine box, smoking his blackened corncob and gazing at the far-off horizon, hardly speaking from one hour to the next. Gulls would fly lazily overhead to see what we were doing. When the fish didn't bite, I'd become bored and restive and want to move on to a new place, but he always looked at me as if I'd suggested going back to harbor.

"We sit right here and wait for 'em," he'd say. "They'll be along soon." And he would nearly always be right. After a time of silence, with the boat rocking gently in the faint swell while we stared dreamily across the bright, glassy blue sea at the islands so dark against the luminous summer sky, the fish would begin suddenly to bite. At once life became so exciting that I would pay little attention to blisters and the hot bite of the line through my fingers. The thrill of landing the big cod and pollock was supreme, and I understood well why Papa would much rather go off fishing on a beautiful afternoon than stay ashore and fix his lobster pots.

In those early years, our bait for a day's fishing was squid, when they were in season. At sunset we went out of the harbor and partway around the island to jig for those strange-looking fish. Everyone used squid for bait in those days, and it was no uncommon sight to see eight to fifteen boats in a big cluster, all jigging for squid. It would be in mid-summer, and anyone who was visiting the island was invited to go squidding, too. Each boat would have a crowd aboard. Boats from Matinicus would join the group, and they would all drift toward each other until their sides touched gently. People would laugh and talk and call back and forth until the squid came schooling, and then the shouting and squealing would begin.

The squid sprayed an odorous black ink the moment they came out of the water, and it was nothing unusual to get hit in the eye. It was always advisable to wear old clothes and peel them off as soon as you got home. If you were a seasoned squid-jigger, you could almost always steer the squid so he would fire on someone else, but while you were diverting him, somebody would be sure to make a target of you.

You arrived home damp and smelly and dirty, but no one really minded. Along with the fun of jigging, you'd had the joy of being out on shimmering, sunset-hued waters. The ride back to the harbor across a sea tinted with violet and rose, aquamarine and gold, was so lovely that it choked you and made you feel breathless and prayerful all at once.

The look of the island in such an hour of calm and color was that of an enchanted land. The rocks seemed more golden as they gleamed in the afterglow; the trees appeared more majestic and proud, rearing against the sky; the open fields had a softer, more spacious appearance. Criehaven is just a small island, but in those moments it loomed high and huge upon the sea. The tiny harbor, with its high, rocky, eastern wall, was a port in a dream when Papa and I came chugging slowly into it in our stubby little boat, powered by a loud staccato motor that made more noise than speed. When the engine was still, the dreamlike hush came over the harbor again, and the hush was as deep as the sea, until the sound of a closing door or somebody's whistle broke it. And then it was something that just breathed around you and you were part of it again.

It was never time to talk while Papa hooked onto his mooring and we tumbled into the dory and rowed ashore. We saved the talking until we got home and told Mama and the rest how many squid we'd caught. She must have been proud of us when we got a lot, but she never seemed to say much about it. I guess that when she took one look at me and my inky face, with my hair all sticky and tumbled and my clothes wet and odoriferous, she could only think of getting me cleaned up immediately.

By the time Papa and I had washed and had something to eat, it would be time to get some sleep for the next morning's early rising. When I snuggled into bed beside Evelyn, who shared my room in the new house, I would go drowsily off into a land where the ocean was forever colored by sunsets, and where the squid were caught without squirting their nasty ink. Before I went to sleep I would think of the squid and how, when you catch them, they look so white and soft and boneless, with their long tentacles covering up their sharp beaks—ugly enough to make you shudder. But as they lie in the bait basket on the way back to the harbor, all the colors of the sunset and the rainbow sweep over them in waves as they die. Then they are beautiful, and you watch them with as much awe as you watched the western sky and sea a little while before.

Getting up in the morning so early that the stars were still bright in a deep, velvety sky and a tiny sickle of a moon hung low in the west, was almost as good as coming home from the squidding ground in the sunset. The air would be so cool and sweet with the smell of spruce and rockweed, and the only sound outdoors would be the low murmur of the sea against the rocky shores. Papa would send me to the garden for cucumbers while he built up the fire and fried eggs and potatoes. We would sit in the quiet, lamplit kitchen while the rest of the family slept. We ate our breakfast slowly, each with an old magazine but with an eye to the lightening sky. I could never forget those mornings; the stillness, the dewy coolness of the wet cucumber leaves as I felt around under them in the darkness for a cucumber big enough to pick. I would be as sensitive as a young animal to all the scents and sounds, the shadows, the starlight, the warm light coming into the east, the glow of the lamp streaming out from our kitchen window.

When Papa and I had finished our breakfast, he'd pack a dinner pail and fill the water jug. We would go to the shore then. I'd carry the jug and the pail, and he'd carry the oilclothes and the extra pair of boots that I'd put on when we got aboard his little old boat.

The morning sun would be coming up from the sea, and everything would be awakening: gulls circling, crows flying up from the woods, songbirds trilling from the alders and wild pear, roosters crowing from the chicken yards. Other people would came out into the morning—fishermen on their way to the shore, most of them going to haul traps, but a few intending to fish for cod and pollock, like Papa and me. Women would go out to the hen houses and pig yards to feed their precious stock. It seemed to me that when the sun came up, flooding the sea and the island with the warm morning light, everyone uncurled like flowers and came out-of-doors to get a good breath of the freshness and fragrance of the air.

The island summers always seemed to be a perfect time. I suppose it was because I had more chance to run around behind Papa. Sometimes I wonder why he was so willing to let me go with him instead of sending me back to Mama and the kitchen. Maybe it was because he knew that I'd probably run off and loaf away the hours on a rocky ledge looking over the sea. Maybe he thought he could at least keep me busy if he brought me along.

Simple Eating ～

Mealtimes, and things to eat, seemed to be of the utmost importance in those early years. We were always hungry. To Papa we must have seemed like so many young birds, our mouths perpetually open to either receive food or declare loudly that we were starving to death.

Papa believed in simple eating. No pies with beaten-up eggs puffed over the top for him; he wanted good, stout pies like apple, mince, squash, and whatever berry might be in season. He liked doughnuts—big, fat ones with crusty, brown outsides and chewy, golden insides. For breakfast, he liked biscuits big as saucers, high and nicely browned and light as a feather, or yeast dough fried in wide slabs in fresh bacon fat, with a bowl of good, strong tea. He liked fish and potatoes with pork scraps, served with mashed squash and Mama's piccalilli. He liked baked beans with plenty of lean pork, and a big baker-sheet of cornbread, and sauerkraut. In fact, he liked everything that was hearty and filling.

He not only liked food, but he could cook as well as most women and better than some. I always enjoyed the hours he spent cooking, and he never shooed us away from the scene of operations as

Mama did. If he made a crock of doughnuts that took him most of the morning to fry, he made almost no comment when they disappeared down our hungry young throats within two days. He might assert mildly that he'd be damned if he knew where we put so much grub, and he'd ask us to see if we couldn't leave a few for his breakfast. But that would be all we'd hear from him.

He'd catch fish and dry them for the winter's table, and then let us eat most of them before they were barely dry, tearing off long strips to chew with stolid delight while we cut paper dolls, read old magazines, or played a version of solitaire with worn cards.

He'd spend weeks over a barrel of sauerkraut, getting it to just the right tartness, dreaming no doubt of the way it would taste with baked beans in the wintertime, and yet he would never stop us from eating it by the bowlful in the evenings, the way children sit with a box of popcorn or a bag of potato chips nowadays.

I think his idea of something to top all delights was to fill a great iron kettle, which Mama had gotten from Grandma, with yellow-eye beans and a big slab of lean pork, the right proportions of mustard and molasses, and put them on to bake early in the afternoon. By eleven at night he would be having a plate of beans—testing them, he called it— and as sure as a whiff of the heavenly aroma came winding through the rooms to us children, we would come out to join him. I can remember many nights in summer when we came home from dances at the clubhouse to find Papa testing his beans. And I can remember how Mama would fret and fuss because we made so much noise in the kitchen instead of going off to bed. But how could anyone walk away from the sight of those delicious beans on Papa's plate? How could anyone shut his nostrils to that wonderful smell? We hadn't the fortitude, and Papa never made us go up to bed. It would seem almost as if he didn't know we were in the kitchen. He'd sit by the big table, with an old magazine at one side of his plate and a bowl of tea on the other, and never look up at us—unless we got into an argument about who got the biggest piece of pork. Then he'd gently say that there was enough for all, and not to be hoggish.

I can't remember any of us getting indigestion from eating a big plate of newly baked beans around midnight.

In the winter, on days that were too stormy for him to go haul his traps, he'd make a dicker with Mama: If she would knit* him some trap heads, he would cook dinner. Mama was a fast knitter—she could turn out twice as many heads as he could—and he didn't like knitting anyway. And as she always seemed to be in the dough-dish, as she called it, she was glad to sit by the fire and knit while the snowflakes whirled and the ocean smashed against the shores. As far as she was concerned, Papa could peel and fry and bake to his heart's content.

In winter, when there were two stoves going, Papa wasn't satisfied to cook on only one. He'd have a kettle of something boiling on the top of the sitting-room stove, and most of the covers on the kitchen stove also would be occupied. Before he was married he'd cooked in logging camps and on schooners, and he was delighted when he could drag all the pots and kettles out from under the cupboard and see the steam bubbling out from under the covers. I liked what he prepared, but it was no fun cleaning up after him, because he used a lot more dishes than Mama did. He used them the way he cooked—in a big way.

Papa used a lot of nice, dry wood when he cooked, too, so that meant that one of us was busy keeping the woodbox filled, but once the table was set and we all crowded around it, we forgot about dirty dishes and empty woodboxes. We just looked at the big, steaming platters piled high, and sailed in. When at last we leaned back, breathing hard with repletion, he would gaze at us solemnly and remark, "Food was made to save life, not to take it."

---

* "Knitting" is the Maine coast term for netting. Lobster trap heads and bait bags are made individually using twine, a mesh board (a gauge to ensure even mesh size) and a "needle" (a narrow shuttle on which the twine is wound).

He liked to have Mama make a big batch of piccalilli every fall; no other pickle was as good with fish and potatoes, he always said. So there was a great deal of onion peeling and slicing, and green tomato slicing, and then the cooking in the big kettles, until the house was practically drenched with the mouth-watering fragrance of the steam. Then came all the tasting and testing to see if the relish had the right texture and sweetness. Papa would stand over it as much as Mama did, and when the moment came to put it in the big gray earthen crocks and cover them well, he would be right on deck to take them out to the big workshop that stood in back of the house.

We had no cellar to keep such stuff in, but the workshop was a good, clean place. The big, wide bench at the back was never used for building traps, since Papa worked at the end near the door, so each fall it was customary to see stone crocks standing back in that dim corner. And each fall it was hard for us to pass by the workshop without pausing, knowing that so much sweet-tasting, pungent piccalilli waited there in the dusky shadows. We knew we couldn't touch it until Thanksgiving—that was the official day for breaking into a crock. But when Mama happened to be gone from the house and a big pan of new biscuits sat cooling on the dresser, how could we resist making a sandwich? Temptation was always too great, and we were always weak. By Thanksgiving, there was barely enough piccalilli to last until New Year's.

After Papa killed and dressed his pig each fall, there was a period when we ate all the fresh bacon we could hold. He never salted anything but the thick, white fat, for salt pork. Sometimes he pickled the shoulders and hams, but not often; the meat was too soon gone.

I see now that he might have rationed things and made them last, but he could never refuse us anything to eat. When a lean time came, and one plate around the table must go almost bare, it was always his plate. But as long as he was able to get the food into the house, there were very few lean times. We always had lobster and fish: lobster chowder, fried lobster, lobster boiled and drenched in vinegar to eat with beans as you would eat pickles; baked stuffed fish, fried fish with homemade salad dressing, fish chowder, fish corned-in-the-kettle. We had little butter. I can remember Papa telling us to eat around a biscuit and save the butter to put on the next biscuit, and then we could imagine we had butter for each one. Fried salt pork seemed to take the place of butter with him. It seemed to go with everything except roasts.

There was one food item that the other islanders ate more of than we did, but only because Papa and Mama were the only ones in our family that would eat it. None of us children liked the strong flavor of eiders, coots, and oldsquaws. Once in a while Papa would shoot a duck for himself and Mama. She would make a stew with dumplings, and we'd turn up our noses at it, but because we saw there'd be nothing else, we'd take a taste of the vegetables and dumplings and get up from the table barely satisfied.

Papa liked to gather berries, and in the summer he would be as eager as any of the women to get away to the pastures with a two-quart pail. But when it came to picking over the berries, he always figured we could help Mama with that tedious job. He'd done his part, and it was up to someone else to do the rest.

I never liked picking berries. I hated the flies and the mosquitoes and hornets and crawling worms. I hated the sun that burned the back of my neck and the heat that came up from the ground when we picked strawberries and raspberries in the summer, but in the fall, when the cranberries ripened, we children enjoyed picking those. There was something about the crisp air, the big, billowing clouds that blew across from the west, the blue-green sea that was stirred constantly into whitecaps, that made us willing to haunt the cranberry bogs and fill the big pails with the hard, sour, red berries. I guess I enjoyed knowing that the cold wind had numbed the bugs and worms more than knowing I was helping to see that we had plenty of cranberry sauce to go with pancakes on a snowy winter evening.

Papa liked molasses cakes with lots of raisins, and Mama made them frequently. But she liked big sugar cakes with thick icing made of brown sugar, and so we had a great many of those, too. When it came to the children's vote, we preferred sugar cake. The frosting was like candy, and we had little candy in those days. Molasses candy and popcorn balls we made at home in the wintertime; at the store we got penny chocolate drops and peppermint sticks when Papa could afford it, but that was not often. For fruit, I remember apples and pears; we didn't have oranges and bananas until I was well grown. Grandma had plum trees in front of her house. The plums were sour and green when we ate them, but they made wonderful preserves. Grandpa had some cherry trees when we first moved from Vinalhaven, and I remember the white foam of their blossoms. But in a few years he had chopped them down because they were worm-eaten.

We had cabbage soup and turnip stew sometimes, and we liked them, and I know now that Grandma's influence extended to their cooking, for there was enough sugar in them to give them a decidedly sweet flavor. We didn't know then that few people put sugar in their soup as Grandma did. But Papa liked it that way, and he liked the way Grandpa fixed salt herring and mackerel with sugar, vinegar, and onions; and he approved when Grandma rolled her slices of fresh fish into flour until they were thickly caked before she put the slices into a chowder.

He liked the bread that Grandma made—big, crusty loaves that made the saliva run in your mouth the minute you saw them coming out of the oven. But when Mama set yeast dough so that she could make a few loaves for us, Papa could not resist using so much of it to make fried dough for breakfast in the mornings that Mama's loaves turned out to be just a pan of rolls. And it *was* hard to decide which way the dough tasted the best, fried or baked.

Woes of a Washerwoman ～

When I was fifteen years old, in 1920, Mama had a very bad case of erysipelas. My youngest uncle, Charlie, went to the mainland for the doctor, and Aunt Ellen came and went frequently and helped with the nursing. Mama was so sick she was sometimes delirious, and the doctor had spread a black salve* all over her face and shaved her head. She wore a kind of mask made from soft white cloth, and she looked very strange in the big bed. The windows of the bedroom looked out over the harbor, so when Aunt Ellen came she could sit by the bed and a window at the same time and watch to see when Uncle Peter came in from hauling. She would go home and get his dinner and then come back again.

At night, Papa helped out as much as he could, and all of us children were remarkably peaceful and well behaved. We all knew, even the littlest of us, that Mama was dangerously ill and that the older people had other things to think of besides watching us. We did all right

---

*Probably a treatment similar to the "Black Ointment" still sold as an herbal remedy. The modern preparation contains leaf from chaparral, lobelia, comfrey, red clover, mullein, and chickweed, root from golden seal, plantain, and marsh mallow, plus myrrh gum, in a base of olive oil, beeswax, pine tar, and vitamin E oil.

by ourselves, proving that we could be quite civilized when the occasion demanded it. After a while Mama was up and around the house, looking very odd with her brown hair so short all over her head. For a long time she had to wear a veil over her face when she went outdoors.

In October, after the sickness was all over and done with, she went to the mainland to have another baby. By now I was through grammar school, and though I wanted to go away to high school, Papa couldn't afford to let me go when Mama needed someone to keep house while she was off on the mainland. Perhaps she would have done better to have hired even the most unskilled of housekeepers. She must have thought so when she came home with the new baby and saw what havoc I had wreaked with my very first washing.

I knew more of the woods and the shores, and much more of the lobsterman's art, than I did of housekeeping. My years of skipping away from household chores had left me woefully ignorant—but I did know that Mama boiled the clothes to get the dirt out. When Monday morning came along, and the other children had gone to school, I was full of good intentions. Papa would know that I was really a clever, capable sort who could do anything to which I lent my hand, whether it was wood chopping or washing. I hoisted the boiler to the stove, put a lot of soap and water in it, and tossed in clothes until I thought the boiler would hold no more. With the stove filled with big, stout sticks of wood, I went off to do something else, feeling very efficient and matter-of-fact.

Once in a while I shoved the boiler over to put in more wood, and lifted the cover to give the clothes a poke with a stick. I disliked putting my hands in water and scrubbing laundry on a washboard, and I figured that the longer I boiled the clothes, the less scrubbing I'd have to do. I boiled them all morning, and just before the other children came home for dinner, I shifted the clothes into a tub with a little cold water to cool them.

After our dinner at noon, I suggested to Ruth that she might help me get the clothes out of the tub before she returned to school. Perhaps

Ruth, always the little housewife, was gratified by my sudden spurt of domestic energy. Anyway, she was glad to help me, and I began to feel very happy as we set to work. There was really nothing to washing; Mama made a lot of unnecessary fuss and work for herself, I decided. My mind leaped ahead with exhilaration to a wonderful project; I would clean the house from top to bottom, putting all the other children into action, and thus would prove to Mama that all she needed was a System...

My daydreams were interrupted when Ruth uttered a small scream of dismay. She was holding aloft a white middy blouse. At least it had been white once, but now it was streaked and lined all over with bluish-gray stripes. It was a good blouse, almost new. But now it would never be fit to wear except to play in, unless we could get the mysterious stripes out of it.

We scrubbed it frantically, but the stripes stayed, and then, with a sense of foreboding, we examined the other clothes. A couple of Papa's best white shirts, some white trousers for Oram, a little white cotton dress for Evelyn, sheets and pillowcases and towels—they'd all been in the boiler, along with a variety of underwear *and* a pair of long black stockings! Those stockings had boiled and cooked, and in my pokings with the stick I had maneuvered them around among the clothes until each article had some mark on it. Ruth's blouse was the worst, but everything else also had stains that would not come out.

I was filled with horror. How could I ever hang up any of those things on the clothesline and let all the neighbors see what I had done? I thought nothing at all about spoiling Papa's shirts so he could never wear them for best again, or ruining the blouse of which Ruth was so fond (she'd gone back to school in tears). All I could think about was the ribbing I'd take from Aunt Ellen and Grandma and the rest when they realized that I'd boiled a pair of black stockings with the white clothes.

Alone in the kitchen, I stood gazing at the tub of clothes. All my fine rapture of the morning had gone, and I was quite sure it would never return. I wondered bleakly what to do with the clothes. Whatever it was, it must be done before Papa came in from hauling, or he would make me string them on the line to blow in the crisp October breeze, out in the front yard where the whole island could see them—and laugh at me.

Behind our house was a little hill covered with scrubby spruce trees. The hill was really a granite ledge, so that the trees grew sparsely in places. In my frantic search for escape, I thought of those spruces. It was seldom that any grown-ups passed through that little, pindling growth. I would hide my terrible mistake there. As furtive as any murderer hiding away a corpse, I wrung out the clothes and took them a few at a time into the shelter of the trees and spread them out on the low branches and shelving rocks where the sun could reach and dry them after a fashion.

Then I came back to the house to face the rest of the washing. It had suddenly become the most miserable drudgery in the world. I was poignantly sorry for Mama, who had to do a washing several times a week—and at the same time, I wished she were home to do this one.

Now I had a fear of the boiler. I would boil nothing. And though I hated scrubbing, I bent my shoulders to the board and went through the rest of the clothes. I could not get them as clean as Mama did; her lines always looked so beautiful, with the white things as snowy as a gull's breast. I put the lighter-colored items on the back lines and saved the front lines for the dark-colored things. If I didn't get them as clean as Mama did, from a distance who could tell? Somewhat relieved, I found that the back lines were enough in the rear of the house so that nobody could see what a poor washerwoman I was, and from across the harbor, when the lines were full, it looked as though I really knew what I was doing.

Papa came in from hauling before I was finished, but he went off to the shore again as soon as he'd had his dinner, and he made no comment about anything, so I breathed easier. The terrible day was almost over.

But along in the late afternoon Aunt Ellen came bustling in. She looked critically at the lines of clothes and was shocked. "Don't tell me you didn't change the beds when you started washing!" she exclaimed. "Your mother'd have a fit!"

She looked at me as though it was the height of sloth and stupidity not to change beds and wash sheets on a Monday morning. I thought of the zebra-striped sheets spread out on the rocks among the little spruce trees and for some reason decided it was better to appear slovenly and shiftless than to confess about the long black stockings.

I shrugged nonchalantly. "Oh, I didn't want to bother with sheets today. I had washing enough as it was. I can do them next week."

I tossed it off casually, but inwardly I was all trepidation and dismay. If Aunt Ellen had noticed the lack of sheets on the line, then every woman on the island had also noticed and put me down as a lazy housekeeper who would let her beds go weeks at a time without changing them. But the die was cast. I shrugged magnificently and refused to confess to a pair of long black stockings.

I didn't realize that when Mama came home with a new little baby girl named Mary Louise—who had big dark blue eyes and dark brown hair and looked exactly like a little doll—I didn't realize that she would find those stained and ruined clothes and demand an accounting. I didn't guess that Papa, who could not afford to buy good white shirts every day or every week or even every six months, would eventually know what I had done, and look at me with wonder, shaking his head and biting his lips.

Worst of all, I couldn't foretell that Mama would not stoop to hiding the sheets in the woods the way I had done. She would boil them as usual, and then hang them on the front lines for the sea winds to blow out and snap vigorously in the face of all those who passed by. And she would not hesitate to explain what had happened to them whenever anyone asked.

A Gentleman's Hospitality~

Because our family continued to grow larger and our living quarters remained small, we were naturally somewhat crowded, and all social life had to be conducted in the kitchen, which was the largest room we had. During mealtime, when the table was drawn out from the wall and we were gathered around it, the kitchen itself had little extra space. What with the stove, and the big rocking chair that was a necessity for rocking the baby, and the tall bureau behind the door, and chairs enough for us all to sit in around the square table, there was just enough room for Mama to get to the stove and dresser and back to the table without being squeezed.

Other families had dining rooms, and their families were not so large that they crowded a room, but we weren't bothered by that fact unless someone dropped in at mealtime and Papa insisted that our visitor sit down and share whatever we had on the table.

Papa seldom bothered with the baby's high chair. It took up too much room. Besides, I think he enjoyed holding the current baby on his lap and feeding it bits from his plate. He didn't hold with Mama's peculiar idea that whatever was on his plate was too heavy for a baby's stomach. Grinning at her protests, he would mash up a baked bean or a bit of fish hash and feed it into the eager little mouth while Mama fussed helplessly.

"Good for him!" he'd say. "It'll put hair on his chest."

We'd all have a vision of the baby with hair on its chest, and we would greet Papa's remark with loud laughter, but Mama never thought it was funny. This made her rather a spoilsport, since the baby always liked what Papa gave it. But we were all shocked—all except Papa, who thought it very amusing—when Russell sneaked Papa's old corncob off the table and crept behind the stove to smoke it while it still held live coals. Russell was only four at the time, and we others expected to see him curling up with cramps, turning dizzy, and being sick all over the place.

Strangely enough, Russell didn't get sick, and Papa said that if it didn't make him sick, it wasn't hurting him any. I was just learning from my high school physiology book that tobacco was terribly injurious to young people—it stunted their growth, along with other horrible things—and I had a mental picture of Russell always remaining the same short, broad little boy who could crawl in behind the stove and stay in the warm chimney corner like a small animal in a cave.

Mama made so much of a fuss after that incident, and kept such a watchful eye on Papa's pipe whenever he left it lying on the table, its pale blue smoke curling up from the blackened bowl, that it was not often Russell could swipe it and crawl away for a quiet smoke.

On the whole, Papa was careful of the things we did, and he was especially critical of our appearance and actions at the table. No matter how dirty and torn our clothes might be from the things we'd been doing outdoors, we couldn't sit down at the table without combing our hair and washing our faces and hands. We could not play with our food, and we couldn't argue with one another while the meal was in progress.

At other times of the day, he could sit and read while we conducted a loud wrangle right under his nose. It would appear that he was totally oblivious of us, even if we arrived at the point where we were pushing each other around. It wasn't until somebody fell into his lap and knocked the book out of his hands that he would suddenly awake to what was going on around him.

"Take your racket somewhere else!" he would roar at us, and subside behind his book again, apparently ignorant of the fact that we kept right on being noisy.

But when the chairs were drawn up to the table for a meal, and he sat down and faced us across it, he became suddenly another person. He would eye us austerely, one by one, and if he saw hands that were not thoroughly scrubbed, he'd scowl and say, "What did I tell you about coming to the table that way?"

There was no point in telling him that the dirt came from tar, or stain from the roots of dandelion greens. We'd tried that. His scowl grew more ominous. "I'm not in the habit of eating with pigs. Get up to that sink!"

And if one of us was in a hurry to get back out of doors to play and made a quick job of eating, his eyebrows would come down dangerously. "Only dogs gulp their food down like that. Are you a dog?"

There were times when we couldn't see any need for such strict measures during meals. We felt that Papa was going beyond our environment. We'd always had to eat in a cramped and steamy kitchen, except for the first few years after we'd come back to the island. That kitchen had been big enough for everything we'd ever needed, but since we'd left it, our kitchens were hardly big enough for cooking and washing. And because Papa could overlook so many other things that some parents wouldn't have endured, we couldn't understand his insistence on what he called "a few manners."

When someone came to our door at mealtimes—whether a grown-up or a child—Papa always made room at the table and told Mama to bring on another plate. No matter how simple the meal might be, even when it was no more than hot biscuits, applesauce, and fried pork scraps, with big cups of steaming hot tea, he was always the expansive host. We used to wonder at him. We knew that almost everyone else on the island wouldn't think of having a meal without some special dessert, and some families always had sliced cold meat, even at suppertime. When we were by ourselves, we children didn't care about desserts and cold meats; it was only when someone dropped in that we looked at our table and realized how much was lacking. And then we looked at Papa, wondering why he, too, didn't feel the lack.

We knew that turnip stew was supposed to be something you cooked only when you had reached the small end of your resources. But we liked it, especially on windy, snowy days when the frost was so thick on the windowpanes that you had to scrape deep with your fingernail to get even a glimpse of the little harbor with its green and white tossing waters and the wildly bobbing boats. We enjoyed turnip stew, with its bright orange bits of turnip, creamy white slices of potato, and tender crescents of onion swimming in a thickened gravy, rich and sweet, with tender, tiny squares of lean salt pork. We didn't mind turnip stew at all.

But if we were caught at the table with turnip stew when someone called, we squirmed in our seats as Papa waved his hand grandly at Mama and said, "Bring on another plate, Agnes. And dish out some more stew."

Fortunately for our juvenile sensibilities, we seldom had anyone dropping by at suppertime, but one night in the early fall of 1921, when we were steadily and soberly making our way through a great platter of fish hash, a knock came on the door.

All the heads came up, all eyes stared at the door. No one on the island ever knocked. Usually the caller simply turned the knob, poked in his head, and said, "Anybody home?"

We all continued to stare at the door, and then Papa called out, "Come in. Come in. No need of knocking!"

The door opened slowly, and for a long instant there was only the black shadow of the night outside showing between door and casing. We were all imaginative kids, and in that moment, with the slow opening of the door after the mysterious knock, the emptiness, and the cold breath of the night, we expected to see almost anything appear, from Rip Van Winkle to the devil himself.

Personally, I was struck by an icy dread. I'd seen a picture long years before, a picture where a half-opened door showed the figure of Father Time, complete with scythe, preparing to enter. Inside the room a little baby lay in its cradle. It was dying, and I knew that when Father Time stepped inside the door, he would take the baby with him... Now I sat rigid in a sort of horror, half sure that Father Time was standing there, even though I knew it couldn't be so.

We looked from the doorway to Papa. He frowned, wondering who was playing a joke on him. "Come in!" he said again.

A face peered cautiously around the door, a long, thin face with a coal-black mustache and eyebrows. It was waxy white, and that alone made it strange, since everyone we knew on the island was deeply tanned by sun and wind. The pale mouth under the sleek dark mustache said softly, "Good evening, Hermie," and then the man himself stepped inside the kitchen and closed the door.

We all let out a long breath of relief, and our eyes lit up. Papa was smiling broadly, and we children were bright-faced with anticipation. We knew our caller. He lived on Matinicus, and his name was John Young, but everybody called him John Tom. He was a quiet man, and given to solitary explorations around the islands.

I thought he was a most romantic figure, with his mustache and eyes so dark against his white skin. He had long, delicate hands, and he always wore dark clothes and a black felt hat. I loved him the way I loved the familiar yet enchanted characters in my storybooks.

Papa motioned to us to move and make room at the table, and Mama brought on a plate. We should not have been surprised to see John Tom. On his infrequent calls he always came at night, and he always knocked. We felt him to be a little superior, he had such manners: knocking at the door, taking off his hat when he came in, sitting down so easily and quietly in his chair.

He nodded around the room to all of us and then came to the table. We were sorry we had eaten so much of the hash, but Mama had outdone herself that evening, and we'd sailed into it with such gusto there was only a bit left. Papa was pushing it all onto John Tom's plate, tush-tushing John's remarks about not wanting it all. Mama brought him a cup of hot tea, and there were still plenty of hot biscuits left.

We all began eating again, but now we hardly cared whether it was hash or sawdust. We were watching John Tom and listening as he talked with Papa. We stared at him, seeing how meticulously he had combed his hair and mustache, how white and clean his hands were, and how neat were his clothes. We listened as he told Papa how he had borrowed a skiff from a man on Matinicus and had rowed to Sou'west Point, the farthermost point of our island, to look for signs of a vessel he knew had been wrecked there many years before. He had taken this day for exploring because it was the time of month when the tide was extremely low, and we could imagine him looking here and there among the long black ledges of Bull Cove Reef, trying to find the spot where the vessel had been tossed in a wild winter storm.

We knew that long, lonely stretch of reef well by sight, but we had never been close to it. We had seen it on our walks around the shore, on days when it was calm and the tide was so low that the ledges lifted from the sea, looking dark and mysterious. When the wind blew and the sea was raging, the reef was a wild tumble of green water and boiling white foam. We knew that only the wild ducks, the shags, the gulls, and the sea-pigeons had an intimate acquaintance with Bull Cove Ledges.

Now we were hearing how John Tom had been rowing in among the bleak, seaweed-covered rocks, hunting for a lost vessel's ribs in the beautiful lilac and gold of the sunset, roaming alone in a wild place while all the other men were home doing their evening chores and getting ready for supper. It added greatly to the romantic aura that we children saw around John Tom. It made him even more mysterious to us.

We knew nothing more of John Tom, except that he had been educated well and lived at home to take care of an invalid mother. He was the one person whom we didn't mind coming to our table in its barest moments. Somehow we knew he never measured us by our substance.

We were as disappointed as he was that he had found no sign of the lost ship. "It would be a great thing to find her," he said sadly. "She was copper-fastened."

We had no idea what copper fastenings were, but because John Tom thought them important, so did we. He stopped talking for a few minutes to eat his hash and biscuits. We watched him carefully, seeing what Papa meant when he told us to sit quietly, keep our elbows off the table, and abstain from stuffing our mouths until we looked like squirrels with a nut in each cheek. Of course nobody else on the island showed very bad manners at their meals, but we knew that Grandpa thought nothing of leaning both elbows on the table while he sipped his coffee from a small white bowl, and there were many times when a man took a quick pause for a mug-up and didn't stop to clean up the way Papa made us clean up. But somehow John Tom, with his look and his manner, was suddenly the epitome of all that Papa had tried to teach us. Perhaps if John Tom had worn overalls and rubber boots, and had tar under his fingernails and untidy hair, and if his face had been tanned and weather-beaten, we wouldn't have paid any attention to him at all.

"Didn't get many fish today, did you, Hermie?" he asked Papa. He was the only person to call Papa that, and we liked the sound of *Hermie*; it was intimate and debonair.

Papa cocked his eye at John under a bushy eyebrow. "No, John, I didn't do very well today. But how did you know?"

John Tom laughed quietly, as if he'd put something over on Papa and it pleased him very much. "I rowed up alongside your boat when I came into the harbor, and felt around." He shook his head. "It's very disappointing, isn't it, to get so few fish for a day's work."

"Couldn't be helped," Papa said in an offhand manner. "That's the way it goes. One day you might do all right, the next day nothing at all, even if you go back to the same spot."

"The fish are nice big ones, though," said John thoughtfully, taking another of Mama's hot biscuits. "You intending to dry them?"

"Thought I might," said Papa. "Want me to save you out a few dry ones?"

"I'd take one of the fresh ones back with me, if you don't mind," said John. "A big fish chowder would go real good for a change."

Papa nodded. "Sure! Help yourself, John. Take two or three and corn them. Make you some good meals."

"No, Hermie," said John. "Just one fish. That's all I want." He stirred sugar into his tea and laid the spoon down carefully in the saucer. The way he did it made us feel ashamed that Mama hadn't put a cloth on the table. Such ease in handling silver merited more than bare wood, even if it *was* well scrubbed.

Papa shrugged his shoulders at John Tom. "Foolish, if you don't take more than one fish," he said.

"No, Hermie, not foolish." The soft voice held a quiet rebuke. "If you had caught more fish, I might take more. But you have hardly enough there for yourself."

"But I can catch more," Papa argued. "Oh, well. You know your own mind best. If you don't want more than one, don't take but one."

We children sat there listening to the polite conversation, imagining John Tom rowing quietly into the silent little harbor, finding Papa's mooring in the dark, and seeking with his white, clean hands through the boxes and barrels to find out how many fish Papa had caught that day. He could have asked Papa when he came to the door, but we knew that was not John Tom's way. He enjoyed seeing the surprise on Papa's face when he told him how many fish he had in the boat.

In a little while John pushed away from the table, wiping his mouth and mustache with a clean white handkerchief. He didn't smoke, so he couldn't join Papa with a corncob pipe. Evidently he had finished his call, for he rose and put on his hat and went to the door. He stood for a moment with his hand on the knob, and looked around at all of us with his meditative dark eyes.

"Good night, all. And thank you, Hermie, for the good supper." He said it gently, and before Papa could say anything in reply, John had opened the door and was gone, as noiselessly and swiftly as he had come in.

A long sigh rose from us children. We had been sitting as quiet as mice throughout his visit. We had been entranced; but now the kitchen was natural again. The lamplight was yellow and soft within the room, and a clatter arose as we moved away from the table. The usual loud argument came up between Ruth and me as to which one of us would wash dishes and which would wipe. Papa settled back with his magazine and pipe, and Mama took Mary Louise out of his arms and prepared to undress her. Evelyn went back to her doll. Oram asked Papa for his jackknife, and Mama told him that if he was going to whittle he'd have to sweep up his own shavings; she'd swept the floor just before supper. Russell was glowering because he knew it was his bedtime. The kitchen was back to normal. John Tom and his magic had gone back into the silence of the night.

Mama was just slipping the nightdress over the baby's head when she said to Papa, "I wonder why he wouldn't take more than one fish when you told him he could."

Papa looked at her gravely over his book. "He didn't want it. And he wouldn't have taken it if I'd tied it around his neck. That's the way he is." He looked down at his book again, and Mama took the baby back into the bedroom. I pushed my hands down into the hot, soapy dishwater in a dreamy fashion while Ruth told me to hurry up and start washing because she didn't want to stand holding a towel all night. I didn't hear her. I was thinking about John Tom, who spoke so precisely and moved so gently, and was content to go softly and un- hurriedly through life. He wasn't selfish or grasping; he wouldn't take more than his share just because it was offered to him freely, as Papa had offered of his small portion of fish.

That was his way, Papa had said. I figured I knew John Tom's way. His was the way of a gentleman.

And then I knew all at once why Papa was so strict with us, not only at mealtimes, but in all the other things he fought to teach us. His was the way of a gentleman, too.

The Sea and Poetry ~

I don't know just how old I was when the island and the sea began to work themselves into my being. When I became conscious of the sensations that welled up in me, clamoring for expression.

I had learned to read more than my schoolbooks when I was still quite small. I used to sit on the arm of Papa's Morris chair and comb his hair while he read fascinating yarns about the Dalton Gang and the James Boys. Combing his thick, graying crop back from his forehead, slow stroke after slow stroke, was a task I performed well. Being able to read over his shoulder made it a joy, until I reached a spot where the bullets were flying. Then I would get so excited I'd forget to comb, and for a long time Papa wouldn't realize I'd slacked up on my job. There we would be, the two of us—long, lean man and chubby pigtailed girl—sitting with our eyes glued to the pages until the crisis was over.

Then he'd remember me, perched like a small, fat pigeon on the arm of the chair, and notice the comb motionless in his hair, and he'd say, "Kind of slacking up, aren't you?" So I'd start combing again. It relaxed him to have his hair combed, he said. I couldn't see much sense in it. I never wanted mine combed; the snarls were always too hard to clear. But I never protested when he set me to work—I enjoyed reading too much.

At first I had to work hard to get to the bottom of the page before he turned it, for then I would never know what happened, because I was not allowed to read the book by myself. (It was too old for me, he said.) But as time went by, I was able to cover the page as quickly as he could, and from that time on it was seldom that he got a story by me. Later I learned to watch where he put the book after reading, so that when he had gone to haul and I had to take care of the house while Mama went up to Grandma's, I could get the book out and read the story for myself.

After a while I discovered the beauty in words and phrases, and began to copy the things I liked into notebooks. When I read something that touched me deeply, I would think about it for a long time afterward. I was twelve when the teacher read James Russell Lowell's "The Vision of Sir Launfal" to us, and we had to memorize the part that begins

>*Earth gets its price for what Earth gives us—*

and goes on after a few lines to ask

>*And what is so rare as a day in June?*
>*Then, if ever, come perfect days;*
>*Then Heaven tries the earth if it be in tune,*
>*And over it softly her warm ear lays:*
>*Whether we look, or whether we listen,*
>*We hear life murmur, or see it glisten...*

I can remember now how those words affected me, their actual physical impact. I was fully conscious then of the beauty of the little island on which I lived; I was deeply enamored of it and of the ocean that stretched seemingly without end on every side. Although I liked winter, I loved the summer more, because I could get out and almost wholly merge myself with the aromatic land, the sea, and the sky.

Summer was a time to feel as free as the gulls that wheeled above, and June was the beginning of summer. It was as the poet had written:

Then Heaven tries the earth if it be in tune...

I could understand that perfectly. I knew just how the sky leaned down over the sea, and gave the sea its own color from morning until night.

Whether we look, or whether we listen,
We hear life murmur, or see it glisten...

The word *life* in that line meant *sea* to me. Whether I looked or listened, I was always conscious of the sea's murmur or its thunderous roar, or of the sunlight dancing on its vast distances. No matter how still the day or night, you could hear the gentle voice of it, and you must wait for the roaring of the gale before you could hear its deepest thunder.

When I was by myself I walked in dreams. I walked with the words I had read and tried to say to myself what was in my heart when, on a windless, shimmering summer day, the blue of the ocean could make me want to weep. I would have such an intense sadness and could never understand why—I would wish I could lay hold of what I saw and keep it in my hand. I would envy the gulls who could fly high above the sea and the islands and see it all in one glance without having to turn an eye and lose what was in their sight a moment before.

I wondered if other people looked the way I did at the rocky points and ledges when the creaming surf was bursting over them—or did they hate the scene because those immense waves were destroying traps or keeping the men from going to haul? I never asked, but I listened, and I found that to most people the island was a lonely place. It was not easy to keep boats in the small harbor. During the storms, the hearts of all the grown-ups were filled with a deep anxiety, for if a boat went, it was not easy to get another. When someone needed medical help, it was no simple thing to go after the doctor—or even if you were well enough to cross the bay on the mailboat, it was not always calm. The trip was a long one anyway; it seemed like an eternity when the boat was pitching and rolling and creaking.

Everyone thought the island was too far out, and people were too conscious of their isolation. I often heard the men griping and saying that the island was the last place God made, and I knew they meant it as no compliment. I didn't realize until I was grown up that although they griped, the island held them, for when anyone went away, it was not long before he came back.

When I stood alone on the high, tawny rocks of Deep Cove on a calm day and stared across the sea toward the small, cloudlike spot on the western horizon that I knew was Monhegan, the peaceful hush that lay over the water was almost like sleep. I liked to think that the ocean was resting, having a siesta in the lazy hours of the afternoon.

But when Monhegan was not to be seen against the distant skyline and the waters between were an immense, raging mass, and at my feet the combers were roaring in, rolling and crashing and tossing spray high on the wind, I thought of the ocean as an angry force, driven by the whip of the wind. Then the feeling within me was one of stifling excitement and wild joy. I could look the length of the island and see the breakers piling up on the ledges outside Sou'west Point, and the flying white foam was the flying white manes of wild horses—horses of the sea stampeding before the storm.

I never felt sad when the ocean was in a fury—only when it was calm and still. And I never linked the ocean with the dreaminess of poetry when it was harassed by the wind; it seemed too much alive then. But as I got hold of more poetry books to read, I found that other people also had strong feelings about the sea, and they had the power to put their feelings into words. I became more aware of the world and the fact that other people existed. Then the little island became a tiny world on the edge of a big one. All the books of fiction I had read had not brought that awareness to me. It had to be a line such as John Masefield's [from "Sea Fever," 1902]:

> *And all I ask is a windy day with the white clouds flying,*
> *And the flung spray and the blown spume,*
> *and the sea-gulls crying.*

or William Bliss Carman's words:

> *And the last tiny speck to fade out and be free*
> *Is a rose-leaf of cloud on the rim of the sea.*

These and other poems taught me that other people loved the sea as I did. They loved it so much that they had to try and express what they felt. They could put into beautiful phrases the dreams and pictures and realities that came into their minds. I could only stand and look and *feel*. I envied them so much that I ached.

It came to me suddenly one day, when I was out fishing with Papa, that he must have a feeling for the sea too. How else could he sit for hours on end with the line motionless in his fingers, smoking his pipe and staring out over the sea with a moody shadow across his eyes? I could stare at the ocean then, too, but I liked it best seen from the land, from up high on a cliff. When I was in a boat to catch fish, I wanted to feel them biting on my line, and I would fret and fidget until Papa turned around and scowled at me.

"I'm not taking you next time if you can't set still," he'd say finally, and that always silenced me. After a while the fish would start to bite, and the excitement of pulling in the big codfish and pollock would more than pay for the hours of boredom I had suffered while waiting for the tide to turn.

But Papa must have had poetry in his soul, and so must every man who could go out there on the shoals, with the island looking so small and unreal against the sky and only the gulls for company, to wait with patience until the fish started biting.

Of course the fish didn't always bite the way we wanted them to. But no matter if we came in with no more than a couple of codfish and behind us a whole day of simply sitting, listening to the water swash back and forth in the bilge, feeling the sun burn on our backs, our eyes drooping sleepily from gazing down into the green depths of the sea. Papa would be as cheerful as though he'd brought in a thousand pounds. Whether he brought in fish or not, there was something else he'd taken from those hours on the water.

I wish now that I had asked him about it. But maybe it was just as well that I didn't. Somehow I must have known that fishing was a quiet business with him. He talked enough to me at other times. Nights by the kitchen fire, when Mama was off to the mainland and I was the only one to sit up with him and read by the kerosene lamp on the table, he could put aside his book and fill his pipe and talk to me by the hour. But during those long, sun-filled hours of silence on the forget-me-not blue sea, he had no words, and no need for them. He had never read those lines by James Russell Lowell. But I guess he didn't need to read them. I guess he was capable of knowing those things by himself.

The Dory ~

Every fisherman on the island had, naturally, a small boat to row from the beach to the mooring where his big boat lay, to carry traps and bait aboard, to row along the shores when he looked for ballast rocks for his traps, to carry herring home from the torching* or seining, and to take in tow when he went on a long trip in his big power boat. Some of the men had double-enders, or peapods; some had skiffs; some had dories. Papa had a fifteen-foot lapstrake dory that was strong and seaworthy yet easy to row.

She was such a beautiful dory to me. She was strong, but she looked graceful, and her nose and bow were shaped just the way I would have wanted a dory's nose and bow to be. She was safe, or I would have been drowned in my earliest youth, and I felt bound to her with the peculiar and enduring kinship that can arise between a person and a boat.

I rowed her many times to distant beaches where the younger

---

*Torching: torch seining for herring (bait fish) at night. The fish, attracted by the torch carried on one of the fishermen's dories, swim into the seine net, which is then drawn up to form a pocket, trapping the catch. Torch seining is no longer legal in Maine.

children and I loaded it with driftwood for our fires. Morning after morning, I rowed Papa to the mooring and pushed off from the beach below the house to bring him in from the mooring when he came back from hauling. If he got up earlier than I did, and I came down to breakfast to see the dory out on the mooring, her reflection clear and sharp in the calm, bright water of the harbor, I would borrow a skiff and go out to take her off her anchorage. Then I would go on jaunts of my own, exploring reefs and ledges, going ashore in the coves for drift-wood and stray pot-buoys.

At night, when the village was quiet, with tired men sleeping soundly, unaware of bright starlight or soft white moonglow, I would slip out of the house and take the dory, rowing toward the mouth of the harbor, flanked by a high, rocky wall on the eastern shore and low, tree-grown, western harbor point on the other. There I'd drift for a long time, watching the stars reflected in the water, or the path of moonlight broad and golden. I heard the constant, eerie crying of the gulls on the distant ledges and was deeply aware of the subdued yet everlasting murmur of light surf on the faraway southwest point of the island. The boats on their moorings were ghostly white shapes inside the little, narrow harbor. The spruces were black and high against the sky as they stood so silent and secretive on the two hills of the island. Gazing at the flat land between the hills, and the houses showing bright in the moonlight, or shadowed in starlight, I would think of words to describe what I saw, and be filled with a kind of awe at the lonely beauty that breathed all around me.

I hated to slip the oars into the water after drifting in silence for so long. The creaking of the oarlocks and the chunking of the oars would seem almost violently loud, splintering the tranquility. I rowed as quietly as I could, trying not to shatter the pure stillness. Back at the beach, I tied the dory at the wharf and went home, wishing that I need make no sound on the beach rocks and so disturb the dream-like stillness.

It would be pleasant to say that I always got back into my bed without being heard, but it wouldn't be true. Mama heard me, inevitably, and roused Papa. Although I told him over and over that I had just been out rowing, my explanation always bounced back at me from a wall of deepest suspicion. Understanding as Papa was in most things, a growing girl creeping out into a mild, still, fragrant night presented a fixed idea to his mind, and he was extremely conscientious about his responsibility toward me. To Mama, rowing around in the moonlight didn't make any more sense than wanting to read books all the time. So I would be questioned over and over, until they both lost patience and accused me of lying. I think they figured that I wouldn't, naturally, *admit* that I'd been meeting a boy, but that I was pretty stupid not to think up a more plausible reason for being out in the middle of the night when everybody else—except, of course, the alleged boy—was in bed and asleep.

I knew it looked foolish to them: why get out of a warm bed and go out into the night *alone?* I couldn't explain it even to myself. When at last I'd gone to bed, and Mama and Papa had subsided with much whispering, and a younger child had waked up and wanted a drink, I would lie there awake, wondering why nobody else wanted to go out rowing in the starlight. Didn't anybody but me realize how wonderful it was on the water, drifting with the tide, feeling the night air cool on one's face, tasting the salt in the breeze, sensing the gentle rocking movement of the dory as the ocean seemed to breathe under the little boat?

Apparently no one else did. And apparently I could not withstand the urge to go rowing on beautiful, still nights, for regardless of what Mama and Papa said, I went whenever the call came upon me. I was considered a stubborn, willful girl, causing worry and having no consideration for my parents, who merely wished to keep me from harm. The harm was supposed to be one or another of the young men on the island. I was old enough to know there was danger in running out at night to meet a boy: Sooner or later the natural element that was in every person would trap me, and I would wish I'd stayed home where I belonged, only then it would be too late.... But no matter how I argued and raged, neither Papa nor Mama believed I was simply out in the dory and the only harm that might befall me was drowning.

Oram was big enough now, at age eight, to have out a few lobster traps, and we worked out a scheme between us where I would row the dory for him and he would haul the traps. I got none of the money from the lobsters, because he could have rowed himself, but I had the pleasure of rowing, and so I was satisfied.

We were quite a pair. I was stocky, squarely built, and going through a phase when I felt horribly overgrown. I possessed an agonized clumsiness except when I was at the oars of a dory. Perhaps that was one of the charms of my after-dark expeditions: drifting in the dory, I felt exquisitely disembodied.

Oram was much smaller than I, a skinny, small-boned, blond boy with a thin, pointed face, an impertinent nose, and eyes that were actually sky-blue—the deep color of an October sky at the zenith. In Papa's cast-off oilpants and boots cut off at the knee, he looked even slighter than he was.

There was a great pleasure in rowing across the harbor in the early morning sunlight with the gulls flying overhead in every direction. There was fun in being caught in the wake of a passing lobster boat while the brisk ripples bounced the dory up and down. I loved the morning sights and sounds: the engines chugging off so steadily, the clanking of mooring chains, the gulls calling, the crows cawing, the lapping of the water on the rocks, the little noisy surges of foam when the boats went out around the harbor point. The sight of Oram's traps coming up through the clear green water caused our hearts to pound with anticipation. It's hard to say which were the crowning moments of those hours.

Oram had fifteen traps, set out in a swath reaching from the inside of the harbor, around Eastern Harbor Point, down Long Cove a little way, and across the harbor to a spot just outside Western Harbor Point. Each morning through the summer, we made our little round, coming back to the lobster buyer's car very proudly if we had a good haul—or slinking back to the beach very unobtrusively if we'd got no lobsters at all.

But when the fall came, we could not go out every morning. The brisk north and west breezes could ruffle up the sea so thoroughly that nobody went out to haul. Even when it wasn't too rough for the boats, it might still be too choppy for the dory. Then we'd mutter about the weather and be very grouchy and watch tirelessly for the wind to lessen. When we thought it might be smooth enough, we'd start for the dory, but if Papa was on the beach he'd holler at us and make us go home again.

One day he sent us back twice, and we grumbled and muttered loudly until he decided that we were quite disrespectful. (He never became harsh until his patience was tried to a very fine point; then he would scowl in his own terrifying manner and speak sharply indeed.) We knew then that there was no more to be said or done, so we wandered off, somewhat subdued. But we still kept an eye on the harbor and the ocean outside, and we kept an eye on him, and when he left the beach and went off out of sight, we raced down the beach and cast off the painter.

We couldn't really believe what he'd told us—that it was no use to haul the traps anyway, because the rough spell had kept the lobsters from crawling and the traps would be empty. We only knew that we had to get those traps hauled. Oram wanted the money, and I wanted the fun of rowing the dory. I knew just how exciting the lifting of her bow and the dropping of her stern would be when she climbed up over a wave and went sliding down on the other side of it.

We kept our heads turned away from the harbor beach where the dories and double-enders and skiffs were tied. We didn't look toward any of the fish houses where the men were busy working on their gear.

We kept looking toward the mouth of the harbor, where we knew we wouldn't get a glimpse of Papa, who might already have caught sight of us and would beckon us back to shore if he could get our eye.

We were pretty well out by the foremost mooring when we heard Papa hollering to us, but we ignored him. (We'd tell him later that we hadn't heard him.) We kept rowing until we came to the line of Oram's pot-buoys outside the harbor. Sky and sea were brilliantly blue, and it was an exciting, exhilarating day. But as soon as Oram caught hold of a buoy with his gaff and began to haul, I realized what Papa had been trying to tell us. I had to keep rowing hard to windward while Oram hauled, or we would have drifted down on the long, rocky ledge of Western Harbor Point, where the surf was smashing without mercy and flying ashore.

We got the first trap aboard with quite a struggle on Oram's part. The dory wouldn't keep still long enough for him to securely plant his feet, and he was as much afraid of falling overboard as I. To our chagrin, the trap hadn't even a baby lobster in it, and the bait bag was empty. We'd been in such a rush to get off the beach that we hadn't stopped for bait, figuring that the bait wouldn't be all out of the bags and would go for another day at least. Oram slid the trap back into the water, and we went on to the next one.

The wind seemed to be freshening, or else I was getting tired and scared. Maybe it was all three. At any rate, the dory seemed to go harder, the waves looked higher, and the oars felt longer and heavier to lift. Oram gave me a hand with the rowing until we came to the next trap, and when we started hauling, I had all I could do to keep the dory in one place. I wasn't even going ahead, though I pulled at the oars with all my might.

In fact, the rocky shore astern of us seemed to be rushing nearer with frightening speed, and the froth and foam of the breakers seemed to be exploding higher into the air. The waves that lifted the dory had caps of white that sizzled and boiled, and when she dropped her nose into the sea, some of the water danced aboard.

Oram was still pulling on the trap, and I hated to tell him to let it go back and give up the job. That would be admitting we were a couple of weaklings, that we were wrong and Papa was right, and that we were just a pair of kids with no sense, after all. I hated more than anything else to ever admit I was wrong. And so I kept pulling at the oars, wishing Oram could haul faster, feeling tight in my chest and queer in my stomach at the sight of the breakers on the point.

The trap came up to the side of the dory finally, but Oram could not get it aboard. The moment he stood on the rising and the dory lay down, water came in—and the way it boiled in was not pleasant to see. No pleasanter was the feeling of the dory when she seemed almost about to roll over, bottom up.

The wind was tossing Oram's yellow hair about his thin, strained face. It needed only a glance between us for me to know that he felt as I did—it was time to admit we weren't grown-ups after all. Not yet. It was time to give in to Papa.

He let the trap go and I turned the dory around, and after a rather wild instant the wind was under her stern and we were racing back into the harbor. We came in grandly, with the whitecaps boiling on either side of us, and almost without effort we grounded the bottom of the dory on the harbor beach. We jumped out quickly, grabbed her painter, and ran up the slope with her.

There stood Papa on the brow of the beach, his corncob in his mouth, his arms folded across his chest, his chin very stiff, his eyes cold and without mercy. He didn't speak as I made the dory fast. Oram took one look at him and headed rapidly homeward—as rapidly as was possible in those outsized boots—without a glance in my direction. I straightened up and started homeward too, without a word. Papa walked beside me, his arms still folded across his chest, saying nothing until I reached the door of the kitchen.

"Wait a minute," he said. "Come out in the shop. I want to talk to you." He said it very softly, but when I glanced up at him, I knew it was no time to argue or explain. So I followed him to the shop.

He looked at me as if he couldn't really make up his mind as to whether I was defiant and stubborn or merely foolish.

He said, still softly, "Didn't I tell you not to take that dory off the beach?"

I nodded.

"And didn't I tell you it wasn't fit weather for you and Oram to go out and haul?"

I nodded again.

"Then why did you go?" There it was, the eternal question: Why? Why did I always feel compelled to disobey him?

There was no use in telling him I had to find out for myself that he was right; there was no use in saying anything. Nothing I could say would excuse me. I stood looking at him, blankly, and his eyes narrowed to the familiar icy rage.

"You know I hate punishing you, don't you?" he asked, still softly. I nodded again.

"Then why can't you obey just once and not drive me to it?" he asked, and his voice rose a little, as if he were ready to cry out in despair.

I didn't know exactly why I disobeyed. I knew I would eventually push him too far and compel him to whip me. I knew how he hated it. But the urge to do some things was so great that in the face of it I forgot everything else, even the inevitable punishment.

He shook his head, sighed, and slowly laid his pipe down on the chopping block. He took a long lath from the bunch leaning against the wall.

"I hate like hell to do this, and you know it, but you drive me to it. Now, take it!" He took me by the shoulder with one big, bony hand and struck me several times across the back with the spruce lath. The lath broke after a few strokes, and he tossed the remaining bit to the floor.

I didn't cry out or speak. I hardly felt the lath touch me. The pain came from knowing that I'd made him strike me when he knew it wasn't going to do me any good. I knew it, and he knew it. Laying the lath across my shoulders was nothing more than a series of futile motions that could carry no meaning for either of us.

He was baffled because I could defy him—to the extent of putting both myself and Oram in great danger—even when I knew the whipping must come. He had to give it to me. He knew of no other way to punish me; he'd been whipped when he had disobeyed his father, and he would have to do the same to his children now.

"Now, don't you get into that dory again until I say you can," he said, giving me a little push out of the shop door toward the kitchen. "You understand?"

I nodded, not because I meant to obey him, but to show that I understood what he meant.

Oram came to me later.

"Did he lick ye hard?" he asked sympathetically.

I shrugged. "Not very," I said casually. "He wouldn't have done it at all, but he was scared we'd get drowned."

"Well, it *was* pretty rough out there," Oram said in an almost grown-up voice. "We better not try it like that again, or Papa's liable to take my pots away from me."

That remark worked when the whipping hadn't. Yes, Papa might do just that. And then, even on fine mornings, there'd be no excuse to row leisurely along the island shores, listening to the gulls and the motorboats and feeling the swell under the bottom of the dory. We'd be stranded like helpless starfish above the tide, left to watch—without living it—the glorious and exciting life of the lobster fisherman.

Helping
Miss Phillips ~

When I was fifteen a new family moved onto the island, and Herbert, the eldest of the three children, became a chum of mine. He was almost fourteen, freckled, blue-eyed, and full of deviltry. He liked rowing in Papa's dory with me, and we spent many a long summer afternoon in the boat that was my heart's delight. He would perch in the stern with an extra oar under his arm for steering, and we would go off across the tranquil water, enjoying to the fullest the sensation of being free in a little shell made of slim, curved timbers.

Herbert and I were hired by a spinster artist from New York to do various chores around the cottage she had rented for the summer. We washed dishes, brought in wood for the stove and fireplace, ran errands, and sat with her by the open fire in the evenings and listened as she read to us from Dumas. Although we were somewhat bored by her reading, since she skipped the bloodiest parts, we enjoyed the fire and the thought that we were getting a taste of how the other half lived, with our feet stuck out toward the burning logs, a plate of fudge between us, and our boss reading in her strange accent.

Miss Phillips must have liked children a great deal, or she would have thrown us out on our ears many times. We could always count on her to see us through a crisis, and any time we wanted to go visiting somewhere else and didn't want our mothers to know it, we could get her to say that she had sent us on an errand to that very place. She didn't pay us very much for our labors—twenty-five cents a week, each—but at the same time we were exempt from chores at home, and that was worth plenty!

It was my job to be at her place every morning early enough to build a fire in the kitchen stove and start the teakettle boiling. She asked me when she hired me if I knew how to cook, and I said no, because I knew that if I said yes, she'd have more work for me to do. I washed up her dishes, swept the floors, and made her bed. (She soon stopped me from bed-making. I was a little too nonchalant about the way I tucked—or didn't tuck—things in at the foot, and sometimes the sheets hung down on the floor on one side and weren't in evidence at all on the other.)

When Herbert came over, he was put to work chopping wood and carrying six or seven pails of water from a spring that was some little way from the cottage. The spring had been dug out and walled up in the side of a high bank where the sea came roaring in during storms, and after rough weather the water might taste a bit salty for a day. A long flight of steps led down from the top of the bank to the spring. Herbert hated the water-carrying job. I would have done it for him without a murmur—Herbert thought Papa's dory was a wonderful boat, and that gave him a special spot in my affections—but our boss insisted firmly that lugging water was Herbert's job, and she wouldn't let me help him.

Miss Phillips would take her paint box and go off by herself until noon, when she would come back and fix up a snack for herself. Toward suppertime, Herbert and I would saunter over the road again, to bring her anything she might want from the store, help her get supper, and wash up the dishes. She was always inviting us to eat with her, and we were always amazed at the number of dishes she could put on the table for the incredibly small amount of food she cooked.

It annoyed us a little too, because the stack of dirty dishes afterward was much too large, we thought.

She asked us innumerable questions about ourselves and the people of the island, and I'm afraid we told her some very tall tales. We in turn asked her questions, as many as we dared, but there was one we asked the most, with a frank and guileless curiosity: Why was she an old maid?

She always seemed a little embarrassed and never gave us a real answer. Perhaps that's why we asked the question so often. Herbert had the temerity to say he didn't see how she could stand being an old maid, and when she looked at him in shocked surprise, he added artlessly, "Gosh, it must be awful to sleep alone on a cold night!"

I kicked him viciously in the shin, because I could see that he had said something she thought was really terrible, but he just grinned at her in his disarming way, and she shook her head at him, murmuring, "Oh, you strange children!"

But she never stopped asking us to eat with her, and she bought Herbert hundreds of shells for his .22 rifle, after we told her that we thought we might be able to shoot a duck for her if only we had some bullets. It never seemed to dawn on her, even after she'd bought quantities of shells and we'd spent quantities of hours hunting for a duck we never seemed to find, that it was almost impossible to shoot a duck with a .22. We spent many happy days plugging away at buoys and toggles and crows, and never hit anything once. However, nobody could say we didn't try. And she never gave us a suspicious glance, no matter what excuse we gave.

It is only once in a lifetime that two cynics like Herbert and I have such an innocent as Miss Phillips at our mercy. Although we were wise enough never to drain dry this opportune fount, we used her in every way possible to further our designs.

There came a day when she announced that she wanted to have a picnic for us and the other children of the island, and we could also invite any grown-up we wished. There was much discussion on our part as to the locale of the picnic, and we finally decided that Sou'west Point would be a good spot. It was the most secluded and the farthest from the harbor. We told her eagerly that Herbert and I could take my father's dory and carry the baskets, pillows, blankets, and water bottles, and that would eliminate all necessity of any other person having to carry something. Everyone could just have a nice walk along the shore and enjoy the sunshine without having to think about sacking provisions over the rocks.

Miss Phillips said we were very thoughtful and kind and assured us that we were dear, good children. She was always telling us that, and it's a black mark against us that we thought she was blind. Telling us we were good never made us want to be better. We simply patted ourselves on the backs and thought we were about as clever as any two young hellions could be.

The time for the picnic came, on one of those flawless, jewellike September days. It was to be a late afternoon affair. Since school had begun by then, we invited the teacher and an older married sister of Herbert's who was visiting the family at the time. Herbert's older brother was a lobster fisherman, and when the time came for us to launch the dory and start out from the harbor, Edgar kindly offered to tow us with his motorboat. Then he suggested hauling a couple of traps and giving us some lobsters to cook over a campfire, and we were pleased about that, because we figured Miss Phillips would think we pulled a lot of weight with the fishermen.

Before Herbert left his house, he had managed to get hold of some cigarettes and matches, and we had planned to have a smoke on the way toward the picnic grounds. That scheme was ruined when Edgar picked us up, but still, we figured we could think of some way to sneak off later and have a puff or two without being trailed by the small fry of Herbert's family or mine. We had the .22 propped up in the stern and were going to make another try for that elusive duck.

The picnic was a huge success. The ocean was like blue silk, spreading far into the distance toward Monhegan. The Camden mountains in the north were soft and mysterious and romantic against the sky. The rocks seemed to have a warm, pale radiance in the sun, and the turf was hot and aromatic. The little island group appeared to be very remote from the mainland, a little world unto itself.

Herbert and I worked hard collecting wood for the fire. We arranged pillows and blankets. We cooked the lobsters and opened cans of sardines, and we pulled the corks from the water jugs, filling tin dippers and passing them around. And all the time, we were waiting for the picnic to be over and done with. There was no opportunity for us to sneak away for a smoke, so we'd have to wait until we were rowing home.

Finally, just as the sun was touching the sea and the gulls were winging in from their offshore feeding grounds, the picnic broke up. We assured the others that they could start right along; we'd get everything aboard the dory and start for home in jig-time. Nobody argued with us. They headed homeward, trailing along the crooked path that followed the edge of the rugged shoreline. In a few moments they were out of sight beyond the nearest hollow, and Herbert and I let out gusty sighs of relief.

Whew! It had been a long chore, and we were tired. We sat down by the smoldering fire, and Herbert brought out a handful of bent and frayed cigarettes. Being in his pockets all afternoon hadn't helped them any, but we smoothed them into shape and lit a couple. We leaned back against a big rock still warm from the sun and watched our smoke drift away toward the water. This was something like it!

Whenever Herbert and I managed to sneak some cigarettes, it was exciting to realize what would be in store for us if we were ever discovered smoking. Our mothers might catch a whiff of us when we got home and give us a lecture, but our fathers would do much more than that. Much, *much* more. I knew I'd get as big a whipping as if I'd been caught in a lie. The danger of walking so close to punishment added zest to living.

But we weren't really worrying today. Our fathers had gone to the mainland for a load of coarse salt to be used for curing fish, and besides that, no one was likely to show up on Sou'west Point at this time of day. We felt as free as the breeze in consequence. Tonight we luxuriated in security.

When our cigarettes were smoked, we piled everything into the dory and pushed off from the beach. The tide was going, and a wide, black line of rockweed marked the entire length of the island's western shore. Everything was tranquil. The sun had gone from sight, but a clear and shadowless light remained over land and sea. Hating to leave such a peaceful spot, we were both silent and thoughtful as we started off. It had really been a good day, and now it was over...

Suddenly Herbert shouted and reached for the .22.

"A duck," he breathed. "Or maybe a seal!" He pointed the gun and fired. The black object in the water disappeared, so we knew it was a seal. I wanted to shoot at something now, and there was nothing in sight but a pot-buoy. Maybe the seal was swimming underwater and would reappear around the point. Why didn't we go and see?

We turned the dory and rowed back. Sou'west Point towered above us, extra high now because the tide was so low. Nothing was in sight. Maybe around the next point? we wondered. I kept pulling on the oars. Herbert crouched in the stern, holding the rifle. Matinicus Rock was clear on the skyline, and the lights were beginning to twinkle across the sea. The outside reefs and ledges were black silhouettes, and the island itself loomed high and black, the spruce trees rising toward the darkening sky. We felt so alone, so remote, that it excited us. Nobody knew exactly where we were. Everybody thought we were rowing toward the harbor with our load of picnic pillows and blankets. Nobody knew we were looking for a seal to show his head against the dusk-shadowed ocean.

Watching expectantly, we rowed along—past Bull Cove, past Schooner Head, past the high, grim rocks known as Brig Ledge and Camp Cove Ledge—until suddenly we realized it was quite dark. The island was a solid blackness now, and stars were twinkling upon the sea in company with the gleaming reflection of Matinicus Rock Light.

And we hadn't seen a thing to shoot at. We paused and had another cigarette apiece, and talked about rowing into Seal Cove to deliver Miss Phillips's blankets and pillows to her. We were so near to it, we might as well.... We had rowed almost halfway around the island, and it was as easy to keep going as to turn around and go back.

Seal Cove was close off our bow, and we turned in there to land and carry our load up the bank and across the field to Miss Phillips's cottage.

She was pleased to see us and insisted that we sit down and have something hot to drink—we must need it, we had worked so hard bringing her things back. We drank the cocoa she made for us and ate some sandwiches, surprised that we were indeed hungry. We hadn't thought of food as we watched for the seal. Then we tore back to the shore where the dory was tied, and had a difficult time getting her off the mudflats where the tide had left her high and dry. We pushed and pulled, working harder than we'd worked all day—a lot Miss Phillips knew about it!—and got our shoes messy and our feet wet. Finally we got her afloat and tumbled in to begin the rest of the journey home.

As we rowed out of the cove in the hushed darkness, we thought we heard the faint murmur of my Uncle Charlie's boat engine. We remembered that we had heard it starting up in the harbor just as we arrived in Seal Cove, but we had thought he was merely putting his boat on the mooring for the night.

We rowed along, talking of the things we didn't like about school, the things we didn't like about the teacher, the things we couldn't fathom about Miss Phillips, and finally we had rounded Wilson Head, which rose tremendously above us against the stars; now we were on the long stretch between Pudd'n Island Bar and Eastern Harbor Point. We were nearly home, and it had been a beautiful trip. Everything about it had been perfect: the feeling of freedom, the welcome we had received from Miss Phillips, the snacks she'd given us, and the knowledge that we didn't have to face a couple of fathers who would fix us with contemplative coldness and say, "Why haven't you been home before this?" No, it was all as it should be, and we lazed along, having a final cigarette before we got to the harbor.

We had almost reached the harbor point when we heard my uncle's engine again. It sounded very loud now in the silence of the early evening, and we realized suddenly that he was coming up on our rear. For a moment we were puzzled about why he could possibly be out so late, and then it dawned upon us, with a nasty burst of reality right in the midst of our erstwhile satisfaction: Uncle Charlie wasn't simply roaming around the island at night for fun—he was out looking for *us*.

We knew now that our families were worried. We hadn't brought the dory into the harbor before dark, and they had sent searchers to find us. My uncle was a cheerful chap, but I knew that his usual ready grin would be absent on this occasion. And perhaps my grandfather was with him, which would make my lecture really tough.

I bent my back to the oars, and Herbert leaped from his seat in the stern to take hold of them with me. We rowed as we had never rowed before, leaving a gleaming, phosphorescent wake foaming behind us, hoping to make the harbor beach before we were caught and taken in tow.

The dory seemed to respond with an eagerness as great as our sudden energy. She slipped over the black, star-spangled waters like a live thing, and I was proud of her all over again.

We could hear the rush of water past her bows, but louder than the rush of water was the sound of my uncle's engine, echoing from island shore to rocky ledge as he passed over Pudd'n Island Bar. We could not see him in the darkness and knew he could not see us, and the harbor point was close now, so close I could feel the little swell lifting us as the undertow pulled in and out from the rocks.

We slid into the harbor and skimmed over its tiny length, bringing the dory upon the beach with a rush, tumbling out to make her fast to a spiling, and then hurrying up the beach to the path, where we stopped to catch our breath. Then we sauntered languidly toward the store, which was brightly lit and full of evening customers. Herbert remembered that we had no matches left, so he went in to get some for his mother. (It would have never done to ask for matches for ourselves.) I stood outside, watching through the window while he went in to make the purchase, and I could see Uncle Eben behind the counter doing up packages and making change.

I waited quite a few minutes for Herbert. He seemed to be in no hurry about coming back out, and I began to get impatient. I heard my uncle drawing up his mooring chain, and then the sound of his oarlocks creaking as he rowed ashore. He would be coming up to the store any minute now. I wanted to be quietly out of the way before then.

A hand reached out of the dark and touched my arm. I gasped and swung around and saw my mother. One glance at her face in the light from the store window was enough. To say she was put out with me is an understatement. I didn't really blame her, but at the same time it was necessary that I make up a pretty good yarn. There would be many accountings to make.

"What are you doing out here?" she said ominously.

I was casual, and vaguely surprised. "Waiting for Herbert."

"You come along home," she said. "Don't you know you two have had people nearly worried to death? Why didn't you come home when the others did?"

"We couldn't," I replied innocently. "We had to bring the dory back, and then take Miss Phillips's things home. We just came from there." I saw no need of telling her that we hadn't walked.

She was only slightly mollified. "Well, you come on home now."

"But I have to wait for Herbert!" I protested. "We have to do an errand for Miss Phillips. She wants him to get something from his mother," I added earnestly. "I don't know just what."

"Well, he can get it by himself. You don't need to go. It's time you were home. Have you had any supper?"

"Oh, yes," I replied eagerly. "Miss Phillips gave us a good supper."

I was ready to wring Herbert's neck. He was standing inside the store laughing and chatting while I was having to talk fast, and I wanted him to know what I was saying to Mama so we could keep our stories the same. It would be just like him to blurt out the fact that we had rowed all the way around the island.

"Well, come on," Mama said, tugging at my arm. I hardly dared to be openly disobedient when she stood so close to me, so I turned and walked away with her, vowing to peel Herbert down with my bare hands the next day. He was a fine partner in crime!

As Mama and I walked away from the brightly lit store, we met my uncle and Grandpa. There were instant recriminations on their side, until she said hastily that we had come home all right, but had gone over to Miss Phillips's place and had just come from there. So there hadn't been any need of worrying after all.

Uncle Charlie was disgusted. He had been searching the whole southern end of the island, in and out of coves, looking for the dory with a strong flashlight. He had shouted and called, and had been afraid we were drowned. Now he was ready to turn me over his knee.

But in all fairness, nobody could really get too mad with us—we hadn't been out in the dory for hours after all. We had been attending to our job, which was waiting on Miss Phillips. I listened to my mother's explanations—angry as she was with me, she was more concerned with calming Grandpa and his mutterings. I breathed a little easier. But still, I wasn't completely assured, for I didn't know what Herbert was going to say.

I found out the next day, after Papa and Herbert's father came home in the early morning. When Herbert recounted the story to *his* family he told the truth, seeing no reason to conceal it. After all, we'd only rowed completely around the island, and most of the journey had been made in darkness with only the black loom of the island to tell us how near we were to it. The ocean had been calm, and there had not been the faintest whisper of a breeze. What could have harmed us?

Herbert's father gave him a sound switching and then came down to the harbor to tell Papa what we had done. Papa came home looking very grim. He confronted me with Herbert's story and told me I had lied to Mama. I hastened to explain that I had not lied to anyone. I had just forgotten to tell *exactly* how we'd come home.

I knew by the way he looked at me that I'd had a narrow escape. It would have been too bad if he had caught me in an out-and-out lie. As big a girl as I was, he would have broken a good, stout lath over my back. But I hadn't lied, and he wanted to be fair. Still, I had worried Mama, and there was danger in being out in the dory after dark, even though I felt so sure of myself. I was still a young one—I didn't know it all yet, and still had plenty to learn.

He stood looking down at me, biting his lower lip, his eyebrows drawn down so that I could hardly see the glint of his eyes.

"You know as well as I do," he said, "that you go out in that dory too much. You sneak off from helping your mother, and I've tried to make you understand that it's wrong." He paused, and I could feel myself tighten up. These pauses of Papa's... "I think you understand," he said gravely, "but you don't intend to play fair. So, I think it's time you stayed out of that dory altogether."

He spoke so quietly that I couldn't believe him at first. Then I stared at him in shocked dismay. Stay out of the dory! It was like telling me never to speak again to a treasured friend. I just couldn't do it!

"I don't want to see you in that dory again for a month," he said. "If you take her off the beach or the mooring, I'll do away with her. I'll sell her and get me a small skiff." I must have been the picture of incredulous despair, for gradually his eyes softened.

"I know how much you think of that dory," he said. "But I don't think you realize what you've put your mother and me through. So, you just think things over. You stay out of that dory and think about what I've told you over and over. Think about having consideration for others and doing as you're told and not as you want to do. Just think about a few things." His eyebrows came down again. His eyes were frosty. *"But stay out of that dory!* Do you understand?"

"Yes, sir," I replied glumly. "But I wish you'd give me a good licking instead."

He laughed. "Why? Because then it would be all over with, and you could start off in the dory tomorrow morning as if nothing happened? Oh, no! I guess this way is best. Maybe this'll make more of an impression on you. A good licking never does."

He turned and walked away from me. I looked down across the sunlit beach to where the dory was tied. She was partly in the tide way, and the cool water was lapping gently at her sides. The water was touching her lovingly, somewhat the way I touched her when I got ready to push her down the beach. Her oars lay across the thwarts, the sun warming their smooth blades. The sea, swelling gently beneath her stern, made her move a little, and she seemed to be nodding to me, almost speaking, almost saying, "Come on—it's a lovely day for a row."

I couldn't look at her. I had to turn my back and go up on the little wooded knoll back of the house, to sit there by myself and cry, and then be furious with Herbert because he had been so foolish. If he'd come right out of the store, we could have kept our stories straight and then we'd have been safe, for Miss Phillips would never have given us away.

I knew what I was going to say to him when I saw him again. It would not be polite. I wouldn't see him until evening, when we were to go to Miss Phillips's, but it could wait, and it would probably improve with each passing hour.

But Herbert didn't show up that evening or for several more days. He was being kept close to the house for his punishment. And when we finally met, we were too saddened by the fact that the dory was out of our reach to get into a fight.

It was a long and wearisome month—a stretch of delightful autumn days when the ocean shimmered and breathed like liquid sapphire, and the soaring and calling of the gulls was actual pain for me. I watched Papa row off to his mooring without me. I saw the dory tied there in mid-harbor like a patient horse; I watched as she bobbed her nose against the beach rocks while Papa put traps and bait aboard, and my heart was like a stone. There was no excitement in waking to the early morning crying of the gulls and the island's cool glisten, no reason to leap from my bed and dress in a hurry so I could take Papa to the mooring and then have the dory for my own use throughout the day. The joy of island living had gone. I was a prisoner—or worse, I was marooned in the midst of a desert.

I waited each day for Papa to be sorry for me, to notice how I moped and never smiled. I waited for him to say, "Well, I guess you've had punishment enough." I waited in vain. I should have realized that although Papa had almost unlimited patience, he also had a clear understanding of the moment when patience should cease and firmness begin.

His firmness lasted the entire month. He never saw, in all that time, that my face seldom smiled. He never heard my deep sighs. He was totally unaware of the state of my heart. But when the long month was over, he looked at me and said, with a funny little grin lifting the corner of his mouth, "Well, do you think you have things straightened out between you and the dory?"

"Oh, yes!" I said.

"All right. Then you can row me to the mooring this morning, and when the tide's right, take the kids and get a load of driftwood. I noticed there was quite a lot of it in Burgess Cove when I came by there yesterday."

When I stepped out into the morning sun with him, there was never such a lovely shade in the ocean's blue; the gulls' crying was like happy laughter instead of woe, and the salty seaweed smell in the air was the best perfume in the world. The feeling of the oars in my hands, the dory's bottom boards under my feet, the sensation—beyond adequate description—as the dory slid across the harbor waters put such joy in my heart that I thought it would swell up and burst.

As I rowed him to his boat, Papa lay back in the stern of the dory and looked at me, his eyes blue and twinkling. When he was aboard, with his oilclothes and box of bait stowed and the mooring slipped, he started up his engine and went out of the harbor, leaving the dory bobbing happily in his wake. I watched him until he went out of sight behind Western Harbor Point and then took up the oars again to row ashore.

I rowed slowly, easily, feeling the oars dipping without sound into the cool, clear water, and thought about the wonder of being in the dory again. I thought about going for a load of driftwood. I dug deeper into the water with the oars, sending the dory skimming toward the beach. I'd get a good load and have it all in the wood house before Papa got in from hauling.

Sights, Sounds, and Words ~

At last I was sixteen, and still I didn't go to high school. I had gotten it firmly into my head that if I didn't go when I was fresh from grammar school, I would have forgotten so much in a year that it would be useless to attempt at sixteen what I had wanted to do at fifteen. It was boring to be around the house with Mama and the younger ones, so most days I wanted to go with Papa and help him with whatever he had to do.

He was still using the little fan-tailed, low-sided boat he'd had for a long time, and he could not always go to haul when the other men did. So, on bright days when it was too windy for him to haul, he went into the deep woods and cut spruce trees for firewood. He was cutting "on the halves"—half went to the man who owned the woods, half was for himself. I begged and teased to go with him, so he got a small axe for me and made me turn the grindstone to get it razor sharp.

I would set out with him in the morning, wading through deep snow across the fields till we got to the woods. We would carry a pail of tea with milk and sugar added and a pail of biscuits, fried salt pork, and molasses. (Some sandwiches!) There might be a couple of doughnuts or some good, firm molasses cake. The wind would rake at us while we made our way across the harbor beach and turned up the sloping fields toward the woods, but as soon as we reached the shelter of the tall spruce trees, the wind would be gone. Only the distant, even roar of breaking waves on the rocks could tell us that the day was anything but peaceful and calm and full of sun.

On days when the trees were too loaded with snow, we would not go into the woods, but as soon as the branches were bare, we would be busy in the woodlot. Papa chopped down the trees, and I limbed them with my small axe and helped him saw the trunks with a crosscut saw. Often he would give me a hand with chopping off the limbs, which humiliated me. I wanted to keep up with him, but he worked so fast and so easily, and he knew just where to send the axe blade. I wanted to stop and watch him for long moments at a time, to see the sunlight leap from the axe and the big clean chips go flying off into the snow, but I could never take more than a quick glance now and then, for the spruce branches were many and thick, and I had to learn how to cut them off clean or else he would make me stay at home.

How much sweeter was the cold, aromatic air in the woods than the atmosphere of the hot kitchen where Mama cooked and washed! And how much sweeter the sound of the surf on the faraway shores and the chattering of the crossbills in the tops of nearby trees than the sound of the teakettle boiling or the rattle of dishes in the dishpan! And how much lovelier the white blanketing snow on the little slopes among the trees, the luminous, delicate blue of the sky overhead, the deep green of the biggest trees, the brighter green of the younger, slender-limbed spruces—how much lovelier were all of these than the kitchen, where Mama was busy all the day, and the children swarmed everywhere, and the windows were so steamed up you couldn't see what was going on outside unless you stopped to rub them off. (And even then, *looking* out couldn't compare with *being* out-of-doors.)

Papa and I chopped wood and piled it up, ate our lunch, chopped more wood, and then went home before the sun was too far down toward the sea. One day was much like the next as long as the chopping lasted, but there was a peace and tranquility about the woods that satisfied a deep hunger in me, although I'm quite sure I had no idea that I was hungry for anything except food. I only knew that the hard work of using the axe and holding to the crosscut saw was in reality no work at all. It was fun. It was fun even when I cut my shin bone and ruined a perfectly good new stocking and had to tie Papa's handkerchief around my leg to keep the blood from running. It was fun even though my shoes were soon soaked through with melted snow and my feet turned icy cold and then had no feeling at all. It was fun even though at night my muscles ached so I could not sleep—until I was hardened to the hours of swinging the axe up and down.

The colors of snow, trees, sky; the shapes of the trees, the stumps capped with snow, the bare-limbed birches that stood so sparsely and whitely among the spruces; the sight of Papa standing before a tall tree, swinging his axe in an unbroken rhythm; the color of the clean new chips, bright pale gold against the snow; the fallen tree with its dark feathery branches spread out and up from the whiteness—those were the things that made chopping fun, and none of them were found inside the warm and steamy kitchen.

The outside of a house might be beautiful to me, but never the inside. It might sometimes be cheerful and cozy, especially on a cold and windy night when Papa let us make popcorn balls and helped us to mold them, or on a damp and foggy night when the Matinicus Rock foghorn bellowed its warning and the wind came around the corners with a lonely, sighing sound. The house was a place to eat and sleep and be sheltered when the rain came in sheets or when the snow was blinding and needle-sharp against your face. It was protection against the sea smoke that came when the winter days were so cold. That vapor seared the lungs like fire. It sometimes was so dense that you couldn't see the boats in the harbor or the woods or even your neighbor's house, and shingles and clapboards and the laths on the stacked traps were all covered with a white frost so thick it was like fur. *Then* the house was a good place.

On such days, the wood crackling in the stove had a sound that equaled the chattering of the crossbills or the impact of Papa's axe against a spruce tree. The song of the teakettle on the back of the stove was as sweet to hear as it was sweet to see the delicate shreds of cloud against the blue sky over the treetops. And the steam on the window-panes was not to be wiped off, for it helped you feel more shut in, away from the biting wind and the vapor that chilled and burned at the same time. The rumble of the big waves on the beach just below the house could not really drown out the plaintive, high-pitched singing of the teakettle; it was just a bass note that gave harmony to the finer sound.

I had learned to knit trap heads and bait bags at an early age. I had teased Papa to let me handle the long, slim, flat wooden needle and the mesh-board, and show me how to knot correctly. Then he gave me a length of twine, which I knotted and unknotted until I could make the knot surely and tightly every time. Then he set me to work on my first trap head, and from that time on I helped with the knitting. But Mama could always use up twine quicker than Papa or I. Her strong, capable hands would be flying, the needle clicking against the mesh-board, and before you knew it, a trap head or bait bag was done and she was beginning another one.

When the night was black with storm or biting with intense cold, knitting was no chore; it was fun. But when the night was fine and clear for skating, with a white moon sailing high or stars burning thick and bright, or if there should be a card party at a neighbor's house, and you knew that a ball of twine lay on the floor by the window, waiting for your laggard fingers—then knitting was a necessary evil that made your head itch and your hands sore.

Knitting was also a lamentably unpleasant chore when you had a book to read—especially when it was a book so irresistibly attractive that it could make you forget you lived on an island and had seen the mainland no more times than you could count on the fingers of one hand. Mrs. Rhodes, who had been my Sunday School teacher when I was small, had a room almost filled with books, and by my mid-teens I had read most of them. I might never have read Kipling, Stevenson, Balzac, and many others, if it hadn't been for that roomful of books, which had never been closed to me from the time I was big enough to walk to the Rhodes farm after the milk.

Near the Rhodes's big house there was a summer cottage called Surfside, which was opened each summer for the Jameson family from Boston—the same mother and two grown daughters, with a young son, who had tried so hard to make a Campfire Girl out of me. They had shelves and shelves of books, and brought new ones each year. I was permitted to read what I chose, and I came and went in the cottage as I pleased. If I wanted to stay unobtrusively in a corner all day and read, no one questioned me—unless it was Mama, when I came blithely home to a sinkful of dishes that had been waiting for me since noon.

There was something about a book that enchanted me—the covers, the endpapers, the print, the way the words looked—the very feeling of a book in my hand gave me a unique sensation. Music caused unusual sensations too, but books were more tangible; you could see and handle them. Music you could only hear, though some kinds of music gave you thoughts and pictures in your mind and caused inexplicable happiness or depression.

If it had not been for Papa, I'm afraid I would have done little reading. Grandpa believed that any book except the Bible was something in which the Devil was definitely active. People who Read Books—Grandpa could say those two words as if they explained the vilest of sins—were lazy and had no mind to work and get ahead. Since Papa liked to read as much as I did, this seemed a very convenient way for Grandpa to convey his opinion of Papa without coming right out and insulting him.

Mama had never been allowed to read anything but the Bible,

and then only the parts selected by Grandpa, so she could not understand the intoxication that seized Papa and me as we sat by the kitchen table at night reading, not hearing what she said to us, not caring how the wind blew or that the water pails were empty and the woodbox needed filling. There were times when Mama's patience would snap at the sight of us so deep in our stories and so far away from her. She would hide our books or destroy them. But she couldn't cure us. We had a disease nothing could cure. We liked to read.

As the other children, one by one, also fell prey to the disease, it was no uncommon sight to see all of us at the table at mealtime, each with a book or magazine beside his plate. To Mama, this was a terrible thing, an unspeakable thing. She would be frantic lest a neighbor come in and find us eating absentmindedly, each of us with our eyes fastened on a printed page. It might not have been so dreadful for just us children to be doing so, but for Papa to be sitting there, stirring his tea until it was cold while he found out who stole the cattle from the Bar Something-or-Other Ranch—*that* was just plain disgraceful.

When she saw someone coming, she would grab books and magazines, swooping down on us before we knew what was happening, and chuck them violently out of sight. Whoever came in would find us all looking around in a dazed condition, like people who have come out of a dark cave into bright sunlight and whose eyes must get accustomed to the dazzle. I used to think she was mean and hateful to try to deprive us of the joy that comes with reading, but now I know that she was only living by her father's teachings. Now she, in turn, was trying to make us understand that which she believed with all her soul was right.

The Cough
Syrup ~

When I was seventeen, and Mary Louise was hardly bigger than a minute, we moved from the little white house near the harbor beach—so near that the spray from the westerly and northerly winds kept our windows dimmed with salt. By means of wheelbarrows and our bare hands, we moved our belongings back to the other side of the harbor, into a big house in the center of the village, next-door neighbor to the house where Ruth and I had known the pleasure of sleeping in the kitchen.

The house we now took for a home had been made long years ago into apartments—two upstairs and two downstairs. It was always known as the Beehive, and many a newly married couple had started housekeeping in one of the apartments. The two downstairs flats had three rooms each, but the upstairs flats had only two rooms each. An attic chamber ran the whole length of the roof.

Papa had rented the two upstairs apartments, and although it was somewhat exciting to be moving into a new place, we thought we weren't going to care much for this abode, which made us feel like goldfish in a square glass bowl. We had no privacy of any kind here. In the other places we'd had nice back yards, with woods to play in nearby. Even the scrawny little spruces on the hill behind the house we'd just left had given us a great deal of pleasure.

But the Beehive was in the middle of the settlement. Along the shore before us were fish houses, and in a semicircle roundabout were dwellings, and each dwelling had windows that stared like eyes, and we knew there were watchful, curious eyes behind the windowpanes. Every time we stepped outside the door, someone would be sure to see us. And as we were full of vitality, strong of will and lung-power, nobody could fail to hear us. We must have provided a good deal of interest in those days: two grown-ups and six self-centered, stubborn, active children with little time for closing a door quietly or going up the stairs easily or coming down slowly. We must have seemed like twenty people instead of eight.

We settled into the Beehive with much gusto, and in a little while we became used to the goldfish-bowl feeling and stopped worrying about the other houses roundabout. The well was very near, and that was a great comfort to me, as I always had to carry so much water. We could see a great deal of the goings-on in the village, and we found we'd been missing a lot by living on the outskirts, as it were.

By fall, Mama was preparing to go to the mainland again. She was expecting another baby. It didn't come until December, so she really hadn't needed to go as soon as she did, but I was convinced that Mama guessed wrong on purpose. The only time she ever had a rest was in the short period just before a baby came. If she went ashore a bit in advance of the event, who could blame her? She enjoyed going up and down Main Street in Rockland, looking in the store windows, visiting ex-islanders who now lived on the mainland. As soon as the baby came, she'd have to think about going home and taking up her burdens again.

So Mama went ashore in the fall, and to make things interesting—if you could call it such—we all came down with the flu while she was gone. So many people on the island had it that some families were totally incapacitated. Volunteers from other families went around from house to house, kept fires going, brought water, and dispensed what little medicine the house afforded.

While we were all down flat with the flu, Uncle Charlie came each day to see us. None of us wanted to eat anything; we were too weak and nauseated. We just lay in bed and thought of nothing but our misery. I was the last to come down with it, and until then I had kept fires going and given drinks of water—and held dishes under chins, for the water came back up almost as fast as it went down. Papa seemed to have a sort of cold with his attack. He coughed all the time, and the flesh seemed to burn away from his bones from hour to hour.

We had little in the house for medicine, but a neighbor told me to cook up some thinly sliced onion and molasses as a cough syrup for him. I made some in a saucepan. It gave him some relief, but he was still so weak he could not get out of bed. By that time I was beginning to feel woozy from so much running back and forth with so little sleep. When I lay down on the couch in the kitchen for a nap, I would get up dazed when anyone called to me.

One night, very late—or perhaps it was in the early hours of the morning—Papa had a coughing spell, and he called me to bring him some cough syrup. The kitchen was in a very dim light, since the little lamp on the table was turned down. But I could see the saucepan on the back of the stove, so I took it, grabbed a spoon from the cupboard, and went into Papa's room. He lay flat on his back in bed. In the half-dusk he looked wasted and wan, his chin and sunken cheeks covered with a gray stubble of beard, his eyes far back under his eyebrows.

He didn't speak to me, just opened his mouth for a spoonful of syrup. I ladled it into his mouth obediently. He had been lying there so silently that he nearly frightened me out of my wits by suddenly sitting bolt upright in the bed and glaring at me. Instead of swallowing the syrup, he made furious motions to me, letting me know he wanted something to spit in. When he had done that, he roared as loudly as any man can roar when he's hoarse with coughing, and pale as weak tea from illness.

"What in hell you trying to do—poison me?"

I stared at him, honestly convinced that he was delirious. I wondered what to do—I had never seen anyone in delirium, and for a moment I was frightened. I thought it was best to appear calm, so I said easily, "Of course I'm not trying to poison you. I'm just giving you some molasses and onion."

"By God, it's full of chips then!" he rasped. "What have you been doing? Dumping the floor sweepings in the pan instead of in the stove?"

"Papa!" I remonstrated. "What's the matter with you? There isn't anything in the cough syrup. You're just imagining it." And I was sure he was touched with delirium now.

"Imagine be damned!" he shouted, and his voice had a little more strength to it by this time. He was sitting up straight in bed, his stiff gray hair tousled every which way and his mustache bristling. "There's something in that molasses, and it ain't onions! I guess I know—you gave me a damn big mouthful of the stuff!"

He seemed so sure, his tone was so positive, that I went back into brighter light and looked into the saucepan. The molasses and onion had cooked down to a dark, thick, and rather nice-smelling mess. But on the top, except for the hollow I'd made with my spoon, there was a crusting of minute, dark particles. I looked closer, horrified. The particles seemed to be dead black ants! Gingerly I scooped out some and discovered to my amazement and relief that they were dry tea leaves.

But how did they get into the saucepan? Certainly I knew better than to put tea into the molasses mixture. I thought back. I had made tea earlier in the evening so that Papa could have a good hot cup. Apparently one of the handfuls had been dropped into the saucepan instead of the teapot. In the dimness of the corner where the stove was,

I could easily have done it, and in my fog of complete weariness, I *must* have done it.

I went back to where Papa still sat up in his bed, staring at me suspiciously. "Calm down," I said. "T'want nothing but tea leaves. I must have dropped them there by mistake when I made your tea tonight."

Immediately he slid down under the bedclothes, making a little snort of disgust. "By God, I knew damn well there was something wrong with the stuff," he muttered.

"Well, you needn't have accused me of trying to poison you," I said in a hurt tone.

"What was I going to think?" he said impatiently. "You try being half-awake and half-dead with a cough like I got, and have somebody come in and damn near choke you to death ramming a spoon down your neck, and then have the stuff feel like chips and shavings and God knows what else. There wasn't much molasses in that spoonful of syrup, I can tell you that! So don't tell me I hurt your feelings by hollering about poison!" He pulled the bedclothes up under his chin, and I stood there looking at him.

"Well, go to bed," he said sharply. "I guess you need your sleep. If you didn't, you might have seen where you were putting that tea."

"Can't I get you anything else?" I asked. He looked bad, so white and thin and old. I realized for the first time that he was not a young man. He was nearly fifty years old, and he was continually having terrible headaches and spells with his stomach.

"I don't want anything else. I'm all right now," he said, and his voice was softer. He'd gotten over his annoyance and wanted me to lie down and get some rest.

The next morning I was unable to get off the couch, and by the time I was able to walk around the kitchen again, two weeks later, he and the children were all over their sickness and getting back to normal. And when Mama arrived, we were all excited and eager to see the little blond boy she brought with her: Oscar Charles.

Salvaged Treasures ∿

The next spring [1923], on an early morning when the air was still so cold that ice formed in the puddles, I woke to hear Papa building the fire for breakfast. I could hear the west wind wailing around the corners, so I knew it wasn't a day for him to haul, but I pulled the curtains away from the window near my bed so I could look out and see if the sun was shining yet.

It was up, but hardly above the tops of the trees that covered the hill behind the Rhodes farm, and it had the pale light that comes on a windy morning in the spring. Ragged bits of cloud skittered across a sky only faintly blue, and the surf was roaring as it tumbled into the coves. I would have snuggled back into bed, but I caught a glimpse of Grandpa hurrying by the house on his way to the shore.

When a man hurries toward the shore on an island, you wonder if his boat is all right, and what he has seen to speed his steps. "What's going on?" I called to Papa. "Grandpa's running to the shore."

I heard him go to the window, and then he said casually, "I don't see him."

"But I *did*," I said crossly, beginning to dress. "He was running. Something's the matter."

"I've got to go to the well for water," he said. "I'll take a look and see." I heard him take the pail and start downstairs.

I went out into the kitchen, which was still chilly, though the fire was crackling merrily in the stove and the teakettle was beginning to sing. I didn't stop to wash my face. I got into my jacket and ran down the stairs and out into the frosty morning. I couldn't see anyone except Papa, pulling the pail out of the well. So I ran down toward the fish houses where I could look out into the harbor. No boats were missing—none was parted from the mooring and rubbing sides with another—so that couldn't have been what made Grandpa hurry. I looked around for him, and found him down on the beach, where I could just see his head and shoulders as he bent over something. I ran down by the fish houses and out onto the brow of the beach—and gasped.

The entire shoreline was littered with the most amazing amount of wood I had ever seen. Great, long timbers, boards, planks, and big, thick squared blocks of wood bobbed in the cold, rough water near the shore. I glanced out toward the moored boats and could see more wood drifting in.

Grandpa was working furiously, dragging wood out of the water and up above the tideway. As I stood there, too stupefied with wonder to move, one of my uncles joined him, and they worked with silent, automatic cooperation, dragging out what they could, wading in after choice pieces, pulling them up on the sand.

It was a gold mine. I had carried too much driftwood in the dory, picking it up from the beaches, not to realize that. Finding stout planks—even one in a season—amounted to a miracle, and here were scores of planks dancing in the surf, wide and long and thick, glistening with newness. I looked back at the house, wanting to go back and tell Papa, yet eager to start at once on gathering in the magnificent harvest. Well, he'd see for himself shortly, and come too. I ran down the beach and began to drag wood into a little pile for myself, separate from Grandpa's.

In a little while more men came, and children. And then I saw that all along the harbor shore there were people working, getting what they could as the wind and water drove it ashore to them. Papa came down in a short time and worked with me. The sun went higher and higher, but I could not leave the treasure the sea had brought. I forgot that I'd had nothing to eat. The excitement attacked all of us like a strong fever.

Then somebody gave a hail: "The whole west side is covered! Must've been a vessel went ashore somewhere and broke up!"

The harbor shores had been pretty well picked by that time, so everybody went streaming across the fields and toward the woods that separated the village from the rocky western shore.

The messenger had shouted the truth. I climbed to a height where I could see the entire shoreline down to Sou'west Point, and the coves were jammed full of new lumber. Eyes were bright and feet were eager as we went running and stumbling through the bushes along the shore, jumping over hollows and little mounds in the earth, and then down upon jagged, jumbled rocks that looked black as coal in the morning light. The tide was going, the wind from the west; the planks and timbers and decking stayed wherever they touched—on rockweed-covered boulders, on pebbly shores. The yellow lumber lay in rich confusion, and it looked like pure gold.

I have no way of knowing how much wood lay on our shores that day. I do know that every fisherman pulled and tugged, carried lumber in his arms and on his shoulders, and piled his loot above the tide mark until the piles became as high as a man's head. There were such stacks on every beach. Where there was no beach, and the wood lay in the rockweed, the men slipped and clambered and got it up to the grass-ground above, in the shadow of the tall, moss-hung spruces.

There were other children and teenagers on the beaches besides me, and we all worked as steadily as the men. We knew the value of what the tide had brought us. We'd all gone after wood, and knew which kind made the best fires for biscuits, which was good to burn for a slow baking. We all knew how disappointing it was to comb the beaches for hardly an armful of worthwhile fuel.

And here was wood that could keep the fires going for a long time to come. Here was wood that could be used to make doorsteps, to repair a wharf, to be used for more things than we could count. All we needed was the strength and the ability to hold on as long as anyone else, because the harder and longer you worked, the more you could pile up in the long, dry grass.

I was borne on by excitement, by the rich abundance of it, until the entire lot was brought to the safety of the ground above high-water mark. At the end of the day I was so exhausted I could hardly eat my supper. I could hardly get into bed. My muscles ached till they seemed almost to scream aloud. I thought I would never be without pain again.

Then came the task of getting our treasure home. We could take our time with that—the crucial period was over. We found that the stuff had indeed come from a big boat, a four-masted schooner that had gone ashore on a ledge to the westward of us, broken up, and been brought to us by the wind and tide.

Among the other kinds of boards, I noticed there was a lot of matched pine, varnished, and I swapped from my pile to get all I could of the matched pine. Papa couldn't see what I wanted with it, and I didn't tell him until I got it home. The long attic chamber could be divided with this matched pine, and a door put in the wall, and on one side of the wall I could have a room of my own—something I had never had in all my seventeen years. I had always had to share my bed and my room with a sister. It seemed to me that if I could have my own room, I would be very rich indeed.

Papa said nothing to stop me, so I enlisted the help of Oram, and we took out a window at one end of the attic. With the aid of a long rope, we hoisted the boards into the attic. He stood below and tied on a board, and I pulled it up. When I had all I needed, I borrowed Papa's hammer, saw, and nails, and went to work. In no time I had the attic divided and a door made.

I put up shelves for all the books I'd been given, which I had hitherto kept in a box under my bed. I found a small table and by main strength and stubbornness got it up the steep, narrow stairs. I got a little spool bed from Grandma, and a chair, and when I finally sat down to my table with the door closed behind me, and knew for the first time the supreme delight that comes in the peace of one's own room, I felt a bit light-headed.

I still had my struggles to keep that room inviolate, for the other children liked it as well as I did. They liked the feeling of height when they looked out the little window over the other houses to the harbor. They liked to go up there on rainy days when I was out and use my pencils and books to play school. Mama appreciated the fact that this got them out from under her feet for a little while, so she never told them to keep out. But for the most part I had the room to myself, and except for the very coldest part of the winter, I had a place where I could go at night and be alone, and read until morning if I wanted.

In the other end of the attic, Mama kept a lot of boxes and small barrels filled with all manner of clothing that she was saving for the day when she had time to make rag rugs. She'd had the collection for years, it seemed, and it was a source of annoyance to me. On cold or rainy days the children liked to go up and dig around in the boxes and barrels for things to dress up in. Never once did they put back what they pulled out, so eventually the place would look as though a flock of whirling dervishes had been doing strip-teases in there, and when Mama came up, as she did occasionally, she would put me to work "neating up the place." I would glower and grumble and try to get out of it, but inevitably I had to bow down and fill up the boxes and barrels with the coats, dresses, skirts, and pants—and each time I swore loudly that it would be the *last* time.

The collection came to be a real nightmare to me. Every time I saw the children dressing up, I would make a fuss about it and try to make Mama stop them, or at least have them put the things back when they were through. But she didn't care what they did—they were having a good time without getting into mischief.

I tried to get her to dispose of the stuff. I told her cruelly that she'd never make rugs because the time would never come. I told her coldly that if she ever did get to use the rags, the cloth would be beyond redemption. I hectored her, I goaded her—but it made no difference. She wanted to keep the old clothes, so she did.

They became an obsession with me. Until...

It was a wicked thing to do, I know that. But I was desperate. I felt as if something would snap inside me if I had to stuff those rug rags away even one more time. Mama had gone to Rockland again, though not for a baby this time. It was only for a few days, but it was long enough for me to get rid of the rug rags.

In secrecy I gathered a number of empty grain sacks and took them up to the attic. With great relish I stuffed each bag with all it would hold and tied the end solid with twine. Then I waited for nightfall. I couldn't finish this in broad daylight—there were too many informants in the family.

Eagerly I watched for the sunset glow to die away, and then I borrowed Grandpa's double-ender, which was tied to his wharf. The wharf was no more than thirty yards from our doorstep. The tide was high, and there was scarcely any wind.

All the children and Papa were occupied—all except Oram. I took him into my confidence, seeing no way out of it. Why he didn't lament the loss of all the things he liked to dress up in, I'll never know. Perhaps the idea of doing something in secret, something in which we might be caught, added a certain spice of excitement to an otherwise quiet and boring evening. He stood away from the side of the house in the darkness, while I tossed the big, fat bags out the attic window and then came down to join him. We carried the bags to the wharf and piled them into the double-ender, and then he helped me row the boat out beyond the mouth of the harbor, where the tide ran full and strong in the darkness, between Criehaven and Matinicus, past Ten Pound and Pudd'n Islands, toward the Wooden Ball and Isle au Haut.

There in the night, with the peapod dipping to the light motion of the waves, I rolled the bags overboard and watched them bounce to the leeward and then disappear into the dark. Then I rowed back to Grandpa's wharf and we tied up the double-ender and went up to the house, where Papa sat quietly reading and the other children were playing at something or other. Nobody missed us; nobody paid any attention when we came in. We had done a good, clean job.

I sat there in the lamplit kitchen wondering where the bags would go. They would float for a long time, I thought, and how dumbfounded and surprised would be the person who picked up one of them!

It was a long time after Mama got home, a matter of weeks, before she noticed the absence of her rug rags. The children hadn't been playing at dressing up because the weather had been so fine and fair they'd been outdoors all the time. But one day she wandered up to the attic—to look around, I suppose, and see whether everything was strewn about for me to cram back into the boxes again. I heard her come up the stairs, pause for a moment, and gasp. Then she cried out.

"My rags!" she wailed. "Where are they?"

Secure in my own room, I listened, feeling rather uncomfortable. I had a definite presentiment that I was going to regret having done something that had seemed very smart and dashing at the time.

"My rags!" she kept saying to herself. "What *became* of them?" She sounded actually heartbroken. Finally she went downstairs to where Papa sat by the table having a cup of tea.

He knew nothing of the rags, and said so decisively, adding that she'd better ask the kids. Suddenly it came to me, as I listened to them, that I couldn't expect Oram to keep it in. Even if he refused to speak, he'd grin and his blue eyes would shine, and she'd know that Somebody had been Up to Something. If she kept after him, he'd have to talk, so I might as well confess now.

I went downstairs, and said abruptly, "I'll tell you where your rug rags are: somewhere between here and Nova Scotia."

Papa scowled at me fiercely. "What! What are you driving at?"

I imagine I looked very black. "It's true," I said. "I cleaned out the attic while she was gone and dumped them all overboard. They're gone, Mama, and you won't have to tell me to put them back where they belong, not anymore. It's all taken care of." I spoke with a great deal more calmness than I felt, for this might be one time when I'd overstepped too far and Papa would take a firm hand. Who knew? He might have had some affection for those rug rags too.

Mama didn't storm. No lightning appeared in her eyes. Instead, she began to cry. "My rags," she sobbed. "The rags I've been saving for all these years!"

"I guess you saved 'em all right," I said in disgust. "They were all worn out to begin with, and then the kids played with 'em until I couldn't figure there was anything left. You wouldn't have got any real good out of them."

"Oh, I could have," she said, tears streaming down her cheeks. "There was a lot of good cloth left in those things. I just needed a little time to work on them, that's all. And now they're gone!" She burst out into grief all over again.

Papa glared at me, and I said hastily, "Look, Papa, you know darn well nobody on the island ever throws away anything they can't use, and if the stuff they gave Mama was any good, why didn't they use it themselves? Because it *wasn't* any good, that's why! They told her it was fine, and she believed them. But most of that stuff was too light for rag rugs, and she'd have to dye a lot of it, and it was mostly cotton, anyway. Nobody makes rugs of cotton."

She turned on me fiercely. "Lots of people make rugs with cotton braids," she said. "Maybe it's not so good as the woolens, but it's good just the same."

"Well, it's too late now." I shrugged, looking much more airy than I felt. "You really can't blame me, Mama. And besides, you can collect some more rags. People will still keep on giving you those things they don't want cluttering up their open chambers."

She looked happier then, as if the thought gave her some comfort. And I guess she finally realized she was as tired of those old things as I was, for she said no more and went off into another room, and Papa went back to drinking his tea.

Home Management ~

We were still living in the Beehive when my eighteenth birthday rolled around, and after an argument with Mama one day as to my usefulness—or lack of it—in life, I decided to go to the mainland to high school that fall. I was desperate enough to want to make an attempt at it, even though I was miserably short on self-confidence as soon as I was away from the island and the boats. One of Mama's brothers lived in Rockland, and she said he would take me to board, though I would have to work for my keep, as the family fortunes seemed to decrease steadily and Papa couldn't afford to pay my way.

I stayed with my uncle for a time, and then left to stay with some of the Crie family—Horatio and his wife, Mabel. Their daughter had been one of my few close friends on the island when their family had lived there; she'd even been a Campfire Girl. Though I was still working my board, I soon learned to call Mr. and Mrs. Crie Uncle Raishe and Aunt Mabel, for they were as kind and tolerant as any relatives could be. They understood the strangeness of this new life for me, and made things as easy as possible for a wild young one who felt an almost physical anguish at being transplanted from the freedom and beauty of a tiny, remote island to the barren, imprisoning boundaries of a city.

All my life I'd scorned the mere thought of mending, ironing, washing floors and dishes, and yet I didn't rebel against doing these things to work my board. I can account for it only by saying that Aunt Mabel had a mysterious alchemy in her manner and a way of understanding my nature that worked a marvelous change in me. Where I had once been proudly happy at Papa's appreciative nod toward the woodpile I'd built up, I was now just as proud and happy when Aunt Mabel praised my scrubbing, mending, and ironing. To have her look at my small stitches (neat at long last) and shining pots and pans with a pleased smile made my heart sing. Once I asked her, "Why do you never tell me I must do this or that instead of saying 'Do you mind...'?"

She answered quietly, "Because I think you'd find far more pleasure in doing things for me because you *want* to, instead of thinking you *had* to."

She seemed possessed of a wisdom I had never before encountered, outside of my life with Papa, and because I was staying in her house, my days at school on the mainland were not the terror they could have been.

I was marked down for a business course; then I could go to work and earn my living when I had finished with school. But as the days went on through the fall and winter and into the spring, I knew I wasn't meant to be a secretary or a bookkeeper. I was absolutely no good in arithmetic, and bookkeeping filled me with horror. At shorthand I managed to keep up with the others, and in typing I could do fairly well, but the thought of a lifetime spent within walls day after day, sitting before a typewriter, handling business letters and taking dictation, made me weak in spirit. Never to see the ocean, the sky full of clouds, sunsets and sunrises across the water, the gulls—I felt as if I were about to abandon all beauty, all breathing, for a life in solitary confinement.

I was pretty good in English and Literature, and the school days were pleasant only because of those periods. I knew, however, that those subjects weren't going to help me earn my living.

Early the next spring Mama told me she expected a baby in June, so I knew I would be busy keeping house for Papa and the others while she was away. School was over the first part of June, and toward the last of the month Mama left for the mainland and I took over the reins at home.

Oscar Charles was now a chubby little blond tyke, hardly tall enough to bump his head against the kitchen window when he walked under it. Mary Louise, the next oldest, was nearly three, a small, round-faced child with bright blue eyes that had a pixie glint in them. The hair that had been such a dark brown when she was born had turned into a soft, pale, silky yellow. Russell came next. At six and a half, he was still short, and I had my moments of wondering whether his clandestine moments with Papa's pipe hadn't stunted him after all. He was oddly somber, while Evelyn was a round butter-ball, a happy-go-lucky urchin. Oram was shooting up but he was still very thin—and still wore his look of unquenchable deviltry. Ruth was skinny too, with masses of heavy, fair hair and big, deep-set eyes like Papa's that could blaze with either fury or delight. Every one of them was high-spirited, sensitive, and fiercely loyal or fiercely inimical, depending on the circumstances. The years in which the Simpson family occupied the Beehive must have been exciting ones for the rest of the village.

Papa was renting one of the apartments downstairs now, along with the two upstairs flats. We had plenty of room to turn around in, although it meant that we had to go outdoors to get to the bedrooms from the kitchen.

Papa worked nights with the seining crew that summer, and sometimes it would be very late when he came home. As I was often sitting up late with a beau those days, I always had a mug-up ready for him when he came in. It was hard work for Papa—hauling traps during the day, catching a nap when he came in, and then going out to seine herring at night. The other men were younger and didn't mind the work and the lack of rest, but I could tell that Papa was very tired. He was less indulgent with his children and spoke more sharply to us when we got into arguments.

Things were not going well for him. His family kept increasing, but his pocketbook grew no fatter. The little sum that he'd managed to put in the bank when Russell was born soon dwindled and then disappeared, and no money had ever been put back. He still had a garden, a pig, and chickens, but it cost more than he could make to take adequate care of his brood in the matter of clothes, shoes, and other necessities. It must have worried him greatly, although I thought little of it then. I had my own affairs to think about and was kept busy running the house while Mama was gone. She stayed away longer than she expected—or than we expected—because Gertrude Margaret wasn't born until July.

There was little leisure for me, and I missed rowing in the dory, going to Matinicus with my beau in his boat, going to haul with him on cool, sunny mornings when the western side of the island lay in dark, damp shadows. I was short-tempered with the children, and they in turn were sometimes hard to manage. Papa, with his worries, seemed to withdraw into himself more than he had ever done. He rarely told us stories now, or laughed with us and teased. The patience that had always been his in abundance was sadly lacking, and he wouldn't listen to anyone's side of an argument. Instead, he spoke severely to us, gave orders like a first sergeant, and scowled fiercely when they weren't carried out. He was like a weary old eagle that has searched endlessly for food for his brood and must return to the nest with nothing. Summer was always the slack time for catching lobsters, and to help with the food bill he also worked on the fish wharf in the afternoons, cutting off cod heads, cleaning out the insides, and tearing off backbones.

We children were supposed to weed the garden, and for the most part it was taken care of. When it came to weeding the beans, however, Oram rebelled. For some unknown reason he hated string beans to eat, but I couldn't see that that should hinder him from weeding the long rows for Papa. Yet Oram insisted daily that he just couldn't stand to weed the beans, and I had to force him into the garden, aided by the short piece of oak lath I kept handy for disciplinary purposes.

One day I noticed him between the rows, behaving in a most peculiar fashion while Ruth worked industriously in another row. I walked toward the garden very quietly, thinking that Oram was about to be punished for lying down on the job. I could hear him muttering to himself, and found him on his knees. People were passing along on the paths, but he paid no attention to them—he was utterly absorbed with his own concerns. I came to the end of the row, where I could see him very plainly, and found him with his hands folded and his eyes closed, his face lifted toward the hot afternoon sun.

"...and, Dear God, I hope we have no more beans to pick," he said earnestly.

"Oram!" I said, really shocked.

Ruth looked over from her row. "That's nothing," she said nonchalantly. "He's been praying ever since we came out here. I think that even though *he* doesn't like beans, he should think about the rest of us. *We* like 'em."

Oram opened his eyes and looked at me with a sheepish grin. I frowned at him in Papa's most terrible manner. "What's the idea of all this?"

"I don't like string beans," he explained artlessly, as if he hadn't been telling me the same thing for days. "And if there ain't any to pick, then I don't have to see 'em on the table. I don't care who else likes 'em—I can't stand the sight of string beans!"

An account of Oram's actions was duly relayed to Papa when he got home, and we fully expected that Oram would receive a lecture. Papa never allowed us to think lightly of food. He had taught us to feel a certain reverence for it when we sat down at the table, and though he would never deny us when we said we were hungry, we were not to waste one particle. When he caught us doing so, he could be very angry indeed.

But for some reason Papa didn't say anything to Oram about the beans. He only looked at him soberly and shook his head, as though he couldn't understand his boy's making such a prayer. But because he said nothing at all to Oram, I felt it was no use to drive my brother again to the garden to weed string beans.

I knew little about making cakes and breads, although I was nineteen years old. Although my cousin Helen had been an accomplished cook for years, as someone was always reminding me, I'd never wanted to learn. But now I felt that I wanted to know how to make at least one cake and a pan of biscuits. So when all the children were out and Papa was away hauling his traps, I would try my hand.

I wasn't very successful. We had no cookbooks, as Papa and Mama knew all their recipes by heart, and I wouldn't ask a neighbor for one. I thought with delicious optimism that if I tried long enough, eventually a good cake and a good pan of biscuits would come out of the oven.

All the time Mama was away I experimented, and nothing ever came out right. But many were the pounds of flour, the spoonfuls of lard, the cups of sugar, the eggs that I wasted. They weren't wholly wasted, however, for the pig became rather accustomed in time to finding a cake or a pan of biscuits in his trough. I managed to keep my experiments a secret, except from the pig. Sometimes I'd be taking the pan from the oven when I heard a knock on the door or a step in the entry, and I'd rush into the next room and shove the hot pan under Papa's bed and come out nonchalantly, closing the door behind me and hoping devoutly that no one would ask what I was baking. No one did, and no one knew that each day I used up flour and eggs and sugar and lard just as furiously as Papa worked to keep them in the cupboard.

I watched Papa when he "threw together" a pan of biscuits, but I couldn't seem to learn anything just from observation. He scooped the sifter into the barrel and came up with it heaping full; he sifted some flour into a bowl and then shook in salt from a heap in the palm of his hand. He measured baking powder the same way, and scooped lard with a spoon to suit his need. No matter how I watched, nothing I tried ever seemed to come out the same way twice. But when his pan of biscuits came out of the oven, they were cloud-light, nicely browned, crisp on the tops and bottoms, and so tasty we could eat them without butter and call them "finest kind."

He put the black kettle of beans in the oven twice a week as usual, and those were the beans that Oram adored, though he disdained string beans. All of us loved Papa's baked beans, but none of us loved them the way Oram did.

We had plenty to eat while Mama was away on the mainland, but I could not admit to cooking anything but the fish and potatoes, or warming the beans, or frying eggs and pork.

Papa didn't seem to mind the fact that I couldn't bake. I had gone away to school for one year and intended to go the next, and that pleased him, though he said very little about it. I knew that he had always wanted me to go away to school, and was satisfied that I would get along all right. He hadn't been able to get much schooling himself—boys on farms in his day went to school only when the winter weather was so bad that they couldn't do anything else. Papa said he wanted all of us to go to school and get an education, so we wouldn't have to work hard with our hands the way he'd done.

But I had to disappoint him. I knew soon that a business course was not for me, and I had started high school too late to change into another course. So, finally and regretfully, I gave it up—regretfully because of Papa—and I went home to the island, where I had wanted to be all the time I was away.

A Literary
Collaboration ~

Getting back to the island after having been away from it for so long a time made me realize that although it was probably the most wonderful, beautiful spot in the world (of which I knew little), I was not much use to either Mama or Papa. The family was growing up. Oram was big enough now to help Papa, and because he was a boy, it was his right that he should take my place. I was now a Young Lady—how I hated the phrase! It meant that I was supposed to keep away from the dory, the axe and saw, the hammer with which I had helped to build many a trap-bottom for Papa. Girls of my age, if they didn't go to work, got married and settled down.

The boy with whom I had begun to go around when I was sixteen was still beau-ing me—he walked home with me from the dances, came to call in the evenings, and listened politely to Papa's long stories as if he weren't wishing that Papa would go to bed and let us have the kitchen in solitude and peace.

Guy was the only son of Alfred, Papa's brother, which made it a more or less family affair. But though I was much in love, I didn't want to get married. Marriage meant children, and I had no yearning for the tiny, helpless things. If I could have borne them full-grown and able to talk, they might have interested me more. But I had known babies since I was five—I could even pin diapers in some sort of fashion at that early age—and somehow I wanted something different out of marriage. I couldn't quite figure what I really did want; I just knew I'd had a surfeit of babies.

When I had been keeping house while Mama was off on the mainland to have Bette [Gertrude Margaret], Papa and I had waged several arguments over the size of his family. I maintained vehemently that a big family was an extravagance. He couldn't afford so many children, and besides, it wasn't fair to Mama to be always tied down to a baby.

He looked at me as if I had lost my mind when I first told him this. I was washing dishes at the sink; he had been reading. When I turned to him and asked quite casually, "Why do you have so many kids, Papa?" he looked up from his magazine as if he didn't understand. But when I repeated the question he laid down his magazine and took out his pipe, and starting filling it. I wiped a half-dozen plates and put them in the cupboard while I waited for him to answer me.

At last he said, deliberately, "You don't just decide how many children you'll have. You have as many as the good Lord sends you."

I glanced at him quickly to see if he really thought I believed him. He couldn't think I went by that old cabbage-leaf theory anymore! He caught my glance and his face turned dark. We both knew what the neighbors thought of his having such a big family. In a small place like Criehaven, it was difficult not to know the neighbors' opinions. It always infuriated him when any slur was cast in his direction regarding the number of his progeny.

"When you get married," he went on, his voice as grim as his jaw, "you'll have children. Probably as many as your mother's had. You come from stock that has lots of children."

I threw back my head. "I guess *not*," I said with conviction. "I guess I want something else besides a houseful of kids. I don't want to

spend every cent I have on kids. And besides, you never can go anywhere or do anything. You're anchored."

"If you don't have children, you'll be turning away from your
mission in life," he argued. "Every woman is supposed to have as
many as she can, or else she's just nothing."

"You don't mean that, Papa!" I cried. "Plenty of women don't
have children, and they do other things. They do good; they're a big
help in the world."

"Well, if they aren't able to have kids," he said, consideringly,
"*and* they can do good works, then they are some good, I admit. But
having children comes first. My mother had a big family, and it didn't
hurt her any. It's only natural."

I looked at him with pity, feeling that he was far behind the
times. Maybe having a big family when there was some way it could
help the parents, instead of taking every cent and wearing down
patience, health, and vigor—maybe there was some sense in that. Papa
had been born and raised on a farm, and he'd gone to work early, like
all his brothers.

But what about the children that sat at Papa's table? Papa was
gaunt and worn with worrying about how to feed them, and Mama
was nervous and half-sick many times, with a new baby coming along
as soon as the last one was beginning to walk. Had any of them been
able to help him make a dollar to pay for the food and clothing that
had to come into the house for them? I had carried water, picked wood,
helped with housework—had any of it been *real* assistance? The only
money that came into the house was what he earned, and it had to
come from the ocean, out of his traps or off a fishline. It came slow
and hard, and it went such a pitifully short way.

This notion of having a big family was old-fashioned, and it was
time that Papa was made to see it. I had a vision of a new baby coming every two or three years until the house was filled to overflowing.

"Where can you expect to put so many kids," I asked, "if you
keep on having them the way you've been doing?"

"There's always room for one more," he said quietly.

"But Papa, you're getting older all the time," I argued, "and money is still scarce. Maybe there'll come a time when you won't be able to work and provide—"

"I expect the older ones to pitch in and help out the young ones," he said stubbornly. "I expect my kids to work hard and get themselves an education, and go to work, and help each other. I didn't have any schooling to speak of, and I've had to work hard all my life. Since I got married, I haven't had much in the way of luxury. But I expect my kids to do different. And they'll have to help each other. That's all." He turned back to his magazine with an air of finality. He didn't want to argue over the question any longer. It was none of my affair anyway.

When I came back to the island, and he knew at last that I was not going to finish school, he reproached me. "*Now* where's your education?" he asked me, scowling. "How are you ever going to better yourself? What are you going to do, if you want to work for a while before you settle down to get married?"

I had an answer ready for him. "I'm going to be a writer," I said. "It's easy. You just think up a yarn, write it off, send it away to a magazine. You get your money, and that's all there is to it."

"Well..." He scratched his head. "You think you can rassle words good enough?"

"Oh, sure!" I was blissfully positive. Sitting down to write was the pleasantest work I could imagine. I liked to read; I could turn off a good phrase; I had a rich imagination—what else did I need? I explained it all to him.

"Look at all the yarns people tell each other," I said earnestly. "Suppose they sat down and wrote them instead of telling them—wouldn't they be just as good as what you read? Of course, I couldn't write about western cowboys or people in big cities, but I could write about the things I know—"

"That's right." His eyes were bright blue, sparkling with interest under his shaggy gray brows. "It's a good idea. And I'll tell you what we'll do. I know a lot of good stories, and I'll tell them to you. You write them down and send them off."

Papa did know a lot of stories. I had listened to many of them in the evenings when I had wished he would go to bed and leave me alone with my boyfriend. My idea appeared to him not as a foolish fancy, but as an eminently sound, sensible plan, because he was a storyteller at heart. He wanted to start working right away.

So we sat down, he with his pipe all filled and glowing, I with paper and pencil. He began to recall a yarn, and I wrote down his words. He always spoke slowly when he told a story, stopping to light his pipe or to look off into space as he remembered, so I could keep up with him fairly well. I can't remember the story he told me then; it had something to do with a murder on a bridge. Or at least somebody thought it was murder, but it was one of those mysterious disappearances, and nothing was ever proved. Anyway, we used up quite a bit of paper, and sent the thing off.

It never occurred to us that the story would be refused. After all, we knew it was just as good as any we'd read in a magazine, so there was no doubt of its success. We got all pepped up over this new venture, and he was as sure as I was that it wouldn't be long before he could take up his pots and just sit back and tell me stories, then watch the money roll in.

We waited eagerly for a reply, and it grew increasingly difficult to keep our tremendous secret from everybody else. (We were going to confound them with the first check.) After what seemed a long, long time, the manuscript came back.

"Sorry, but we cannot use it." That was what the little note said. Papa and I were stunned. Then we got mad. What did a magazine want, anyway? At last, we knew the bitter truth: Editors didn't just want fine writing. No, you had to have pull. You had to be on the inside, or you couldn't expect to sell anything.

Who wanted to do business with a stranger, anyway? After all, there were plenty of people who were personally known to the magazine folks—naturally, they got first chance. Sure. It was like looking out for your next-door neighbors. When you saw the bait boat coming into the harbor with a load of herring, you sent somebody over to tell the fishermen who lived out of sight of the harbor so they could come and load their dories. If you had a pretty good-sized pig to kill off in the fall, you passed out a taste to your neighbors. It was the natural thing to do. You helped out those who were near to you.

So we knew we had to give up the golden dream that had nourished and enveloped us while we'd been waiting to hear about the manuscript. It was a severe blow to us both. We didn't sit down again to make up stories by the kitchen table after the children were in bed, with Papa's pipe sending up spirals of smoke while he thought up a good line.

But I didn't put the paper aside for good. The writing germ had attacked me a long time before, and I had many notebooks in which I kept my thoughts. I continued to keep those notebooks and to buy others and fill them. It was a long time before I sent away anything of my own, and when I did, it came back. Nonetheless, the joy of putting down words of my own thinking and phrases of my own making was something I could not turn from, and the joy of reading words that other people have put down on paper remains for me as strong as it was when I first discovered the enchanted world that exists between the covers of an interesting and well-written book.

Papa knew that I was still writing, and occasionally he would ask me about it. I hedged around and said I was copying things—which was true. I copied things that appealed to me into my notebooks. He would nod and say no more. He knew as well as I did what kind of nut we'd tried to crack. It didn't occur to either of us that it might have been our writing technique that was at fault—we were too ignorant— but we never ceased to envy the fortunate ones, the lucky ones, who were neighborly with the magazine people.

Music from the Heart ~

It was long before my time when the men of the island who were musically inclined would gather together and practice marches and waltzes under the leadership of a young minister who came to the island every summer. On pleasant days they gave band concerts from the wide piazza of his home, which sat on a rise overlooking the harbor. I have imagined many times how it must have felt on those quiet summer afternoons when the harbor water was like soft, smooth silk, the boats lying at anchor as if they were half asleep, and then the stirring, bright music would ring out over the little village, awakening echoes from the high, red rock cliff of Eastern Harbor Point. I like to think how Papa must have looked, poising his cornet in his long, work-roughened hands, waiting for the moment to begin. I like to think how he must have enjoyed those hours, in company with the other fishermen who cared enough for music to try to give expression to it.

It was long before my time, too, back in the days when Mama and her brothers were in their adolescence and their days were full of the chores that Grandpa could always find for them to do, that they also had the longing for music and the making of it. So, in early spring they muffled their noses in scarves against the stench and went out to pluck the wool from the carcasses of sheep that had died in the pastures during the winter. It took fortitude and strength of purpose to work at such a task and save the precious pennies thus earned to buy an organ.

It was one of the old-fashioned kind, with the little shelves and book rack, and a mirror at the back so you could see yourself when you were playing and pumping away at the pedals. The organ stayed in Grandpa's parlor, where the curtains were never pulled up to let the sunshine in to fade the woolen carpet or give a gleam to the horsehair-cushioned chairs. Even when Mama and her siblings were grown up and had homes of their own, the organ sat in that dim parlor, until one day when Grandma decided that Mama might like to have it in her house.

It was a grand day when we saw the organ coming in through the kitchen door, and the men sliding it across the threshold to the room where Ruth and I had our bed, a folding couch that could be made into a sofa in the daytime. It was exciting; it gave quite a lift to our family pride to know that Mama could sit down and play hymns for us. Papa had sold his cornet long before, when the band had broken up, and I had always felt sorry about that. But now Mama had the organ in her own house, and we could stand around her and give our hearts and voices to all the hymns she knew how to play.

The organ went with us to the little house on the other side of the harbor, and because I was so fascinated by the tones that came from it, I could not let it be. I must pump away and poke out tunes by ear. Then someone showed me a few simple chords that sounded really majestic, especially when you pulled out all the stops. Little by little, I found other chords and learned that I could produce quite an effect with them when I sang the melody. The organ gave me a lot of enjoyment—until the day when I became curious as to what the inside must look like. Being alone, with no one to stop me, I pulled the instrument away from the wall, took off a narrow board, and was amazed at the array of little felted hammers, all placed so carefully in rows.

I reached in and poked one, and even now I don't know what happened to it. All I know is that from that time forward the note played continually whenever you pumped the pedals. The organ was ruined. Who could enjoy trying to make tunes when one note kept playing by itself as if an invisible finger held down the key? The family's eloquent disgust was nothing compared to my own grief. I had spent many delightful hours making music, and now they were ended.

A few months before I ruined the organ, Papa had brought home an old fiddle that he'd taken in payment for a small bill. It was a very bare and forlorn instrument, and I couldn't see why Papa had taken it instead of money. But he said he guessed it was a good fiddle, and laid it away on the top shelf of a cupboard. I took it down and looked at it several times, but it held no interest. It had no pegs, no strings, no bridge, no tailpiece, and no bow. It was just a scratched, unadorned, useless shell, and no good to anybody as far as I could see. Papa had certainly lost out.

I had heard plenty of fiddle music. Papa's older brother, Alfred, had a fiddle and had played at the clubhouse for dances. Lorea Jameson, the same one who had tried so valiantly to make a Campfire Girl of me, brought a fiddle with her when she came summers to the island. Her playing was far different from Alfred's. She played music that was sweet and haunting, and tunes that I had never heard; but they had no meaning for me because they seemed to have no rhythm. I liked music you could waltz by, or do a square dance to—still, I enjoyed the tones she brought from her violin, so sweet and clear with a sort of shimmering of sound.

A French-Canadian family, just come from their native place in Nova Scotia, moved into one of the apartments in the Beehive. They were an exotic group in the midst of our rather conservative island community made up of Yankee and Scandinavian stock. And what made them more exotic—for me—was the fiddle that one of the boys played. He could make the strings fairly dance as he played jigs and reels for the dances at the clubhouse. I played chords for him on the piano, and those dances were truly happy times for me. I enjoyed every part of the evening: the sound of all my neighbors and friends having such a gay time, the lamplight shining on the smooth, broad floor, sprinkled lavishly with corn meal to make it slippery. I liked the music that Georgie and I made between us, and I admired the way he sat so much at ease with the fiddle tucked under his chin, his fingers seeming barely to touch the strings, his bowing arm moving so effortlessly.

One day I asked him if it had been hard to learn to play like that, and he shrugged and grinned, and said no, it was easy. The careless way he tossed it off, as if the dullest of nitwits could play, touched me. He was seventeen and so was I. If he could play so well without knowing a note of music, then I could too. After all, I had the fiddle. All I needed were the bow, pegs, bridge, tailpiece, and strings.

Whether Papa gave me the money to send away for those things, chosen from the mail-order catalog, I can't remember. But they came, and then, to my amazement, Papa took them and put them on the fiddle, tuned it up, and began to play. His fingers were stiff, and he made mistakes, but I knew that at some time or other he had played on a fiddle and knew how all the jig tunes should go.

I began sawing away. From the other side of the house I could hear Georgie's fingers dancing delicately over his strings, and I knew it would be a long time before I could make the same kind of music.

After an hour of my scraping and sawing, Papa could stand no more, and he sent me out of the kitchen. I took the fiddle to the attic and vowed to stay there with it until I could play a song he could recognize. It was "Home, Sweet Home." And when the time came that he did recognize it, I was very happy. All I needed to do was keep sawing on the strings until my fingers knew where to go by themselves.

As the months went by, I realized that I would never be the fiddler that Georgie was. But by that time I had found a certain joy in making music for myself, and the sort of music that Lorea played became more attractive. It was not for dancing; it was the kind of music that made you see pictures in your mind, that described moods and fancies and had nothing to do with jigs and reels. Her music came from the violin the way it was written on paper, and her knowledge of it came from studying—not the way Georgie and I knew it, from hearing tunes and scraps of melody that lingered in our minds.

Papa took the fiddle occasionally and played it for a bit, but he never took it down for himself, only if I'd laid it down on the table for a moment. He would watch me through his pipe smoke and nod appreciatively as I continued to improve, without saying a word of encouragement. I suppose he was wondering when I would do something to ruin the fiddle the way I'd ruined the organ. But the organ had taught me a lesson: One must never, never tamper with the insides of musical instruments.

The little old fiddle that came into our house so bare and mute is still with me. Many times when I am playing on it I can see Papa sitting in the corner of the kitchen smoking his old corncob, eyeing me with a quizzical expression, as if he knew very well that I should be washing the dishes or ironing the wash just in from the lines instead of wasting sunlit hours trying to play "The Devil's Dream," "Turkey in the Straw," or "In the Gloaming."

Changing Times ∾

In those days [the late 1920s] lobstering was not the lucrative business that it is now, and for a long time Papa had been thinking about getting into something different. Lobsters seemed to get fewer and fewer, and the price seemed to get lower and lower. His boat was not very rugged, and he was fighting a losing battle. He told us finally that he wanted to visit his brother in Bucksport and see about moving our family into the old Simpson homestead. He had farmed once; he could be a farmer again, and all the children could help.

A new environment is always of consuming interest to children, and from the fascinating stories he'd told of his boyhood, the youngsters were sure that the old farm would be a wonderful place. So he took Ruth with him on the trip to see his brother Reuben, and the younger children waited with excited confidence for his return. Every hour, the place and its prospects grew in splendor, especially for Mama, whose tattered nerves rebelled at the island's ceaseless winds and the senseless brutality of the sea, which gave out nothing but surf and storm and empty traps.

But when Papa returned, the verdict wasn't good. The old farm had been abandoned for so long that the woods had reclaimed the meadows. The house was in bad condition, too, and Papa had no money for the animals and farming tools he would need. He seemed very thoughtful and sad when he came back, but the disappointment in Bucksport didn't stop him from deciding to leave the island.

He said he would get himself a job. The family would live in Rockland, and the children would be able to go to school and learn many new things; it would be good for them to see something besides an island. Privately I thought it hadn't hurt Ruth and Oram and me to get our grammar-school education from the books in the tiny schoolhouse overlooking Seal Cove. We had all entered high school and hadn't been cast down by any limited education.

It was not a wise move for Papa to make. Having never known anything at all of city life, Papa was no judge of what lay before him. Even though there was no possibility of Papa's being able to rent a more satisfactory house on the island, the Beehive was still far more comfortable than a cheap rent in the city. He would accept no criticism of his plans, however, and could not believe that nobody would hire a man of his age. He was honest and willing, and that was all that was necessary to get a job.

So he sold his little old boat, his traps—all the things with which he had worked for so many years. Oram had now come to an age where he had a boat of his own and a good string of traps, and Papa sold Oram's gear, too, and moved the family to Rockland.

I was married by that time, to the boy who had not, obviously, been discouraged by Papa's long stories. So I stayed behind on the island with Guy and watched them depart, all smiling, all confident. I cannot go into detail about the utter disappointment of the next few months, the terrible attack on Papa's pride. He found out that nobody hired a man so close to sixty who knew nothing but lobster fishing. And the country was so full of unemployed men that the government had to feed their families and find them work to keep them going.

By the time Papa realized that he should never have left the island, there was no way for him to return. It cost a vast amount to get started in the lobstering business, and he had nothing. He would have had to get unlimited credit, and that was hard for anyone, let alone an older, unknown man with a big family of young children.

The day came where he gave up completely to despair, and it was a terrible thing to look at him, to see the lost, lonely expression in his eyes. I couldn't help him; Guy and I could barely scrape along ourselves. There was nobody to help Papa. Even before he had realized entirely that he couldn't find work and that Mama must earn the week's pay by washing other people's dishes and scrubbing other people's floors—before that time, he became the father of another boy—Neil Everett [born in March 1930].

Before Neil was very old, Papa had a slight shock that made him walk with a limp, and bothered him when he tried to talk. He had always stood so tall and straight, as if he were a soldier, and he had always loved to talk—to enchant us with endless stories, to advise us with dignity and a fine flow of language. Now whenever I saw him, I felt sad for a long time afterward. He still had the look of an eagle, but it was an old, tired eagle who has gone far from his eyrie and was too worn to fly back.

It made my heart ache to see the lusterless eyes and the shaking hands that had once taught me how to catch fish, drive nails, make cleats for trap doors, how to row without tiring myself out in the first ten minutes.

Papa was bothered with extremely high blood pressure, and the beating in his ears gave him no rest. It grieved me when I talked with him and saw the younger children playing about the shabby rooms. I knew that, to them, their father was not the proud and gentle eagle who had led me through a trying and stormy childhood—a childhood that would have been infinitely bleak and lonely without him. Their memories of him would never be like mine, and I wished with all my heart that there were some way I could give them those memories to cherish.

I wanted them to know that this querulous, white-haired man with the faltering step and mumbled speech had once been strong and wiry and quick on his feet, sharp and keen of eye, full of stories and laughter, and tender as a woman when he rocked his babies to sleep or comforted them when they awoke from bad dreams.

I wanted them to see him as I saw him, and know him as I knew him: a kind and loving father, an understanding friend.

His health became so bad that he was finally taken away to a hospital in 1935. To the doctors who cared for him, it made no difference whether he was a rich man or poor; they did all they could for him. They told Mama it would be a long time before he could go home, so she took the children and went back to the island to visit Grandpa for a little while. Grandpa was living alone, as Grandma had died many years before [in 1930]. And in May, when Neil was five years old, Mama received a telegram from the hospital, saying that Papa had not survived two severe shocks.

It was a bad time for us all, though it was good to see his children coming back to the island from their new homes. Ruth was married and lived in Rockland. Evelyn was married and lived in Hartford. Oram was working on a freighter out of New York and Portland. The rest of us were there on the island, the younger children with Mama at Grandpa's, and I in my own house.

I could not go to the funeral. I could not go into Grandpa's sitting room and look at Papa. The younger children—Bette [Gertrude], Oscar, Neil, and Mary—didn't go to the funeral either. They stayed with me, and as my house was within sight of Grandpa's, and we could see the road leading to the cemetery, we watched the little group as it left Grandpa's house and walked slowly along. They would have to pass through the woods and the orchard before they reached the gates of the little cemetery.

It was spring, and ordinarily springtime filled us with new energies after the cold and windy days of winter, but spring smells and sunshine could not cheer any of us then, even though we knew that Papa would never have been able to recover. The only thing that could give us any particle of comfort was the fact that Papa would not be buried on the mainland. He had come back to the island he had loved so much, and which had been his home since he was a tall, lean boy of nineteen with a fine yellow mustache. He had come back to the place where the open reaches of the sea had been inspiration for his long hours of serene thought, where the surge on the rocks had sounded loud enough at night to waken from his sleep and make him wonder if his little boat was safe on her mooring, where the stars and the northern lights had made beauty for him on his way home from the seining grounds.

So he was laid away in the little cemetery where the tall, dark spruces hold peaceful shadows and the neighboring apple trees give off their faint sweetness in the spring. But in the sleeping and waking dreams of those who knew him as a gentle eagle, he returns again and again.

⌒

Aunt Dot's Later Life ∿

Dorothy Elisabeth Simpson

S o what happened to Aunt Dot and the rest of her family after her papa died? I can only give a brief overview, of course, as it would certainly take another whole book to show just how full her life was. The journals that Aunt Dot continued to keep throughout her life have helped me fill out the story, and I have also drawn on the recollections of my family and Aunt Elisabeth.

Dot's mother and the younger children stayed on at Carl Anderson's house on Criehaven after Herman died. Agnes later married another Criehaven fisherman, Fred Wilson. She and Fred remained on the island until Fred became ill, and then moved to the mainland in the 1940s. Agnes died in 1955. Dot and her mother had never been close. Perhaps the unrelenting work of bearing and raising so many children meant that Agnes had little time for her oldest daughter. For her part, Dot early on rejected the idea of spending her adult life on endless housework and child rearing. Much later, after Agnes was gone, Dot told me that she eventually came to understand better why Agnes was not able to see beyond a very limited and conventional horizon.

Aunt Dot had married a childhood friend, Guy Simpson, on

December 1, 1927, several years before her father died. Guy was the son of Alfred Simpson, Herman's brother, and thus was a cousin by marriage but not by blood. "Dot had always known Guy," Aunt Elisabeth recalls:

> Guy's mother and father were an older couple—quiet— and Guy had been somewhat of a surprise. He was slight for his age, looked delicate—but wasn't—and had a soft voice. He was five years older than Dot, and on her first day of school he'd defended her against the teasing, the pulling of pigtails, and so forth.... Guy was not sent to high school. No matter how many teachers and learned summer people were convinced that he was bright in mathematics, his parents wanted him to remain on the island. Much as he longed to go, he'd been an obedient son all his life. But he did marry Dot without mentioning it to his parents first.

Sometime around 1935 the couple realized that Dot would need to work off-island to bring in some additional income, so she went to Camden, where she had heard that a woman needed household help. Can you imagine Aunt Dot now going to work doing the one thing she had always tried to run away from? Well, it was a job that brought money into the household, and that was all that mattered. Besides, she was not skilled in anything else at the time.

To her surprise, Dot found that she actually enjoyed her time in Camden. She soon realized that this was an opportunity to develop herself. Here she was introduced to music, art, and a social life that the island could not offer. She inhaled all of the wonderful experiences as if they were life-giving air that she might not encounter again. Guy often came across from the island. Being a naturally sociable person, he appreciated having a reason to make frequent trips to the mainland. Dot continued working in Camden for about three years, until Guy's mother became ill and she had to return to Criehaven to help care for her mother-in-law.

In 1938 Guy had the opportunity to fish the territory around another island in outer Penobscot Bay—a very small, rock-covered bit of land called Wooden Ball. He and Dot spent the 1938 season there fishing and lobstering. Why the island is called Wooden Ball is a mystery; there were no trees to speak of, and wood was in short supply. Dot and Guy had to forage the rocky shore for firewood to heat their two-room living quarters. Because the house was literally set on top of the rock ledge, it was at the mercy of any foul weather. Aunt Dot kept a journal during their stay, and I found it to be interesting and wonderfully descriptive.

After their stay on Wooden Ball, they moved to Matinicus Island for a while, then returned to Criehaven around 1940. To lessen her mother's burdens, Dot had Agnes send Oscar, Bette, and Neil to live with them. I remember Aunt Dot telling stories of these years. There were good times, of course, but never a shortage of bad times too— whether from sickness, lack of money, boat troubles, or uncooperative weather. No matter what the obstacle, the family always found a way around it. In Aunt Dot's writings I have come across many stories of their adventures after they moved back to Criehaven.

The Younger Siblings

Around 1942, Dot's oldest brothers all decided to enlist before they were called up for the draft. Oram joined the Coast Guard; Russell and Oscar enlisted in the Army. Eventually Bette (Gertrude) signed up for the WAVES. It was difficult to have so many of the family off to war, but they kept in touch as often as they could. I found many letters from Oram, Russell, Oscar, and Bette among Aunt Dot's things. They often wrote of their love for the island and how much they enjoyed Dot's letters filling them in on the family and island life. Each spent about four years in the service, and once the brothers got back home it was not long before they were married and settled back into the routine of fishing, as their father and grandfather had done. Bette also returned to the midcoast area, but she married and settled on the mainland.

Ruthie had gone to high school on the mainland around 1925.

During her stay in Rockland, she boarded with a family and was tutored by a gentleman neighbor. Although he was twelve years her senior—and engaged to someone else—he and Ruth fell in love and got married as soon as she graduated from high school. They eventually moved to Florida.

Evelyn also attended high school in Rockland, met someone, married, and moved to Connecticut. She and Ruth returned to Criehaven for vacations.

When Mary was around twelve, she was adopted by their Uncle Charlie and his wife, who had by then moved to Matinicus. This was when her name was changed from Mary to Madelyn. Herman's family was so poor at the time that he and Agnes must have decided to send Madelyn to live with relatives who had no other children and could better afford another mouth to feed. I have been told that Madelyn looked very much like her Uncle Charlie's mother—both had Scandinavian features. Madelyn was very smart, and this was supposed to be an opportunity for her to go to the mainland and continue her education. Her experience with her new family was not as pleasant as it should have been, however, and she could not wait to get away once she turned eighteen. Instead of getting an education, she had to stay on Matinicus and do housekeeping for her uncle and aunt. She met and fell in love with a young lobsterman, and they married and settled on Matinicus. She raised her family there and remained on the island until her husband retired and they moved to the mainland.

Dot's youngest brother, Neil, was my father. He too was a lobsterman. Although he also several times tried his hand at different jobs on the mainland, his heart and spirit were always drawn back to the island, the sea, and the freedom of being his own boss. He married young, at age twenty, and raised his family on Criehaven. I was born in Rockland in November 1953 and taken to Criehaven in December. My parents stayed on the island until 1985, when they decided it was time for my dad to retire from the lobstering business and move to Tenants Harbor, on the mainland

Moving to a New Island

By 1944 things were changing on Criehaven. Dot and Guy were ready to move someplace where they had a better chance of buying a property of their own. Coincidentally, Dot's longtime friend Elisabeth Ogilvie was also looking for an island property. Thanks to the great success of her first novel, *High Tide at Noon*, Elisabeth was in a position to buy something, but had not found a house that appealed to all of them on Criehaven, or even Matinicus. Then, one day, a real estate broker showed Liz and Dot a property on Gay's Island, just off Pleasant Point in Cushing, and that was all it took. By the time they walked away from Gay's Island that day, they'd fallen in love with all it had to offer. So Aunt Dot, Guy, Aunt Liz, and Liz's mother, Maude, prepared to move to another island, only this time it was just a stones' throw from the mainland instead of many miles offshore. Gay's Island is where Aunt Dot spent the rest of her life and where she rests even now.

In 1950, Aunt Liz wrote *My World Is an Island*, depicting their lifestyle and many adventures on Gay's. (It was reissued by Down East Books in 1990.) She and Aunt Dot loved their new home, and at first Guy did, too, but several years after the move, Guy could not deny his feelings of homesickness for Criehaven. It was at this time that he and Aunt Dot separated amicably. It was months before either of them thought about making the separation permanent, but eventually they did get divorced.

Until her death in 1998, at the age of ninety-three, Aunt Dot continued to share her time between the house on Gay's Island, in the warmer months, and a winter house that she and Elisabeth co-owned on Pleasant Point, just across the gut from their island home.

Aunt Dot's Creativity

Despite the magazine editors' brusque rejection of her earliest professional writing attempts, Aunt Dot continued to write fiction, poetry, and short stories. She also kept up with her journals and even composed songs. Aunt Elisabeth recalls how Dot filled notebooks with songs and poems that she liked, writing them first in shorthand, then typing "immaculate copies":

> She composed music for the poems and played them on her Sears Roebuck guitar, and the [island] children learned them and sang with her. She wrote stories of island life, and she kept them private, but all the while the island was being set down on paper. [She also started to paint,] and it was a great wonder to find herself describing the island and sur-rounding waters in paint and with music and poetry."

Through her relationship with Elisabeth, Dot continued to improve her own writing ability. She completed a correspondence course on creative writing. She submitted short stories to many well-known magazines. Finally, her dream came true when Lippincott published her first book, *Island in the Bay*, in 1956 (reissued by Blackberry Books in 1993). She had written about what she knew and loved best: her life on Criehaven.

The inspiration for the book, a young adult novel, came from the adventures one of Dot's brothers had as he learned about lobstering while living with his Norwegian grandfather. Her next four books— *The Honest Dollar* (1957), *A Lesson for Janie* (1958), *A Matter of Pride* (1959), and *New Horizons* (1961)—were also for young adults and all featured a character named Janie Marshall who was much like Aunt Dot herself. *Visitor from the Sea* (1965) was also about Janie's family, but a younger sister, Becky, was the main character, along with a won-derful dog that came to the island as a result of a mishap at sea.

Dot wrote these books so her family would know about life on the island. She also wanted her nieces and nephews to know what her papa had been like. Because he died before any of his grandchildren came along, it was very important to Dot that she share her memories of him. The stories about Janie and her family were, in essence, about herself, the oldest of eight siblings growing up on Criehaven. I can re-member how much Aunt Dot loved to talk about her papa and the island. I always looked forward to hearing those stories over and over again when I visited her.

The Maine Islands in Story and Legend (1960; reprinted by Blackberry Books, 1987) was also a departure from the Janie Marshall series. It was written for a general audience, though young adults would also enjoy it. Anyone interested in the Maine islands should curl up with this book of history and legends—including tales of murder, buried treasure, faithless lovers, and ghosts.

Aside from her writing, Aunt Dot also painted. She wanted to recreate the colors of the ocean and sky that surrounded Criehaven, the island she had come to love and cherish over the years. She had been introduced to colored pastels in her younger years, and when those were thrown away, she needed to fill the void somehow. The Ogilvie family had helped her do this. Maude Ogilvie was a wonderful artist, and she became a mentor to Dot while they were still living on Criehaven, teaching her new ways of producing different effects on canvas. When Dot could not afford to buy acrylics and watercolors, she would use odds and ends of the paint the fishermen used on their lobster buoys, diluting or mixing colors together to create her own palette.

She worked very hard on her painting, and it took years of practice before she was finally happy with her creations. She painted for herself and for family, and occasionally had a commissioned sale. On April 27, 1982, she had her first exhibition ever, at the *Courier-Gazette* newspaper offices in Rockland—a proud day for her. Some of her paintings remain in the family today, while others are spread around the state of Maine and beyond.

Later Years

Along with taking care of the Gay's Island property, Aunt Dot continued to write, paint, play her instruments, and whittle thousands of small buoys and assorted other treasures I have come across. She and Aunt Elisabeth made two trips overseas to Scotland, where Elisabeth was doing research for her novels. Dot also helped with typing up the notes for Elisabeth's many novels. In *My World Is an Island* Aunt Liz described Dot's indispensable assistance:

> Dorothy, who has an equally light hand with a guitar, a boat, and an apple pie, passed on to me the history of Criehaven from its earliest days of settlement, as told to her by her Yankee stepfather and Norwegian grandfather; she typed manuscript for me, and listened to my endless laments about my inadequacies as a novelist, and discussed situations that could or could not happen on an island like Criehaven.

Always an active person, Aunt Dot savored life until she drew her last breath. She liked to cook, despite having gotten off to such a rocky start in the kitchen during her younger days. She also loved to read, and to knit trap heads for the local fishermen and the Friendship Trap Company. Once she reached her nineties, she could no longer play her instruments or whittle, but her passion for music and handicrafts never diminished. We often talked together about the days when she would sit with my father, she with her fiddle or banjo and he with his guitar, and play the great country-western songs of the 1940s and 1950s. Growing up on the island, you learn to make your own entertainment, and for generations of my family, that included singing and teaching ourselves to play a variety of instruments. We always had a great time, and we made some wonderful memories.

I always sensed what a remarkable woman Aunt Dot was, and not long before she died, I thought about what a great loss it was going to be when she left us—not just for me, but for everyone who had spent any time with her. She had a spirit that, to me, was a gift. Just as she wanted to keep her papa's memory alive for his grandchildren, I want to keep her memory and childhood adventures alive for her family.

She originally titled this memoir *The Gentle Eagle*, and indeed the story does often focus on her beloved father. I believe she succeeded in capturing his essential character. So it was when Aunt Liz referred to Dot as "the island's true child"; in that phrase she captured Aunt Dot's essential character. In her own writings, Aunt Dot preserved the essence of how it felt to be an island child eighty years ago and more.

It is with great pride and joy that I share Aunt Dot's words with you. Opening the pages of this book, you stepped back into a world that today can be reached only through the gateway of Dorothy Simpson's faithfully recorded memories. I hope you enjoyed the journey there as much as she and I did.

Afterword~

Elisabeth Ogilvie

Dot Simpson spent most of her first three decades on Criehaven; my family came just for summer visits, but we found ourselves indelibly marked by the island and its people just the same.

One of Dot's first memories—and perhaps the dearest, to have remained so fresh and vivid in her mind even in her ninetieth year— was of being a very small child picked up off the floor by a very tall man, who swung her up to his shoulder, told her to hold on, and then carried her out into a sunny, windy morning. Water was breaking on the rocks, the spray flying at man and child, and both of them were laughing. Arriving at the workshop, he built a small fire in the old round stove to take off the night's chill. Close to his boots she played with scraps of lath and blocks of wood. The fire snapped, the gulls called, the man whistled and sometimes sang—tunes and words she started to learn even before she could really talk.

Dot's earliest memory, then, was of her earliest loves: her new father and her island home. Ever since the time when she played on the fish house floor beside her stepfather's boots, the man and the island merged into one for her, and were together in her heart until her last day.

According to Ogilvie family lore, my mother's first statement on arriving at the island after a rough and smelly trip on a naptha-fueled launch was, "I wish I hadn't came! I wish I hadn't came!" She was six at the time, and she heard that story repeated for the rest of her life, or for as long as anyone else from those days remembered it.

I don't remember my own first boat trip to Criehaven; I was only two and must have slept during the sometimes boisterous twenty-five-mile crossing from Rockland. What I do remember from that first June day was that I'd never seen so much ocean in my life, or seen—and heard—so many gulls. The sharpest memory is of sitting on cushions at the Cries' Hillside farm, suddenly becoming aware of a plate of saltines on the table before me, and being wildly hungry. Everybody was being very quiet, and I broke the stillness by asking my mother for a cracker. "In a minute" she whispered, and then I realized that Uncle Fred Rhodes was speaking quietly, with his hand over his eyes. Suddenly he thanked God in a loud voice, put down his hand, and said, "*Now* you can have a cracker!"

I'm sure it did not take long for me to venture outdoors into the clear summer sunshine, one of many children who over the years played on the island's red-gold rocks or among the young spruces at the wood's edge.

For a child, the island held many wonders, and Dot was one of them. Oh, all the visitors and writers we got to know—the scholars, the dedicated school teachers. We learned from all of them. But Dot was the prime influence. She was eager for greater knowledge herself, but we knew she already had all of it that mattered. Dot, the fiddler, the poet and songwriter, the great storyteller, the historian, the quick wit—she carried the soul of the island within her, and she passed on what she could, including her devotion to Criehaven.

Kin-Folk

God in his glory made the Sea,
And laid it under the sky,
That gulls might wheel and climb and be
White bits of foam that fly
And wing and drift and follow far
The whimsies of the gale,
To touch my heart and the sadness there
As the sight of a distant sail
Disturbs the calm of an old, old man
Who sits with his pipe all day,
To follow the flight of the wheeling gulls
And dream of the salt sea-spray.

That old, old man and I are kin,
And dreams are what we know;
Dreams of the sea, the sky, the stars,
And gulls that wheel and go
On with the wind o'er crag and bay—
Winged bits of the ocean's foam,
Far from the land—down to the sea,
That forever calls them home.

⁓

Dorothy Simpson

Selected Bibliography ～

Published Works by Dorothy Simpson (all originally published by the J.B. Lippincott Company, Philadelphia)

Island in the Bay (1956; reprinted 1993 by Blackberry Books, Nobleboro, Me.) young adult novel

The Honest Dollar (1957) young adult novel

A Lesson for Janie (1958) young adult novel

A Matter of Pride (1959) young adult novel

The Maine Islands in Story and Legend (1960; reprinted 1987 by Blackberry Books, Nobleboro, Me.)

New Horizons (1961) young adult novel

Visitor from the Sea (1965) young adult novel

FOR FURTHER READING:

Fischer, Jeff, ed. *Maine Speaks: An Anthology of Maine Literature*. Brunswick, Me.: Maine Writers and Publishers Alliance, 1989.

Hayes, Melissa, and Marilyn Westervelt. *A Mug-up with Elisabeth: A Companion for Readers of Elisabeth Ogilvie*. Camden, Me.: Down East Books, 2001.

Ogilvie, Elisabeth. *My World Is an Island*. Illustrated By Paul Galdone, N.Y.: Whittlesey House/McGraw-Hill, 1950. Second edition with epilogue and photos, Camden, Me: Down East Books, 1990.

Aleda Dorothy Knowlton Simpson (1905–98) was the author of seven books about Maine islands and their people. She also was an important behind-the-scenes collaborator with popular Maine novelist Elisabeth Ogilvie. At her death, Dot left behind several unpublished works that eventually came into the possession of her niece and namesake, Dorothy Elisabeth Simpson, who was surprised to find that one of those yellowed manuscripts was this poignant memoir of her aunt's childhood in the tiny community of Criehaven on Ragged Island.

In *The Island's True Child,* Dorothy has rounded out her aunt's story by adding an introduction, a concluding chapter, a selection of photographs, and a personal note from Elisabeth Ogilvie. Dorothy also plans to get more of her aunt's previously unpublished works into print.